THE DOCUMENTARY FILMMAKING MASTER CLASS

Praise for *The Documentary Filmmaking Master Class*

"What Betsy Chasse doesn't know about documentary filmmaking can fit in a thimble. She understands that a film must be compelling, enlightening, and visually stunning. In our current day, when everyone with an iPhone and a drone thinks they're a filmmaker, Betsy will teach you how to actually be one."

—Howard Cohen, co-president, Roadside Attractions

"Betsy is in a filmmaking class all of her own. Not only will her methodical yet straightforward instruction establish the foundational knowledge necessary to succeed, but her wisdom and wit make every page a real treat. This is a book to read and reference again and again."

—Trina Wyatt, founder and CEO of Conscious Good and founding director of the Tribeca Film Festival

"Rarely do you find a book with just about everything you need to become knowledgeable about making a documentary film. Betsy Chasse is an expert in this field and has put together a book that is truly the master class you need if you're going to make a film."

—Jonathan Blank, producer and director, *Sex, Drugs & Democracy*

"This book is a must-have for anyone considering making a documentary. The information provided is almost impossible to find in one place, if anywhere, and from someone whose experience and wisdom is invaluable."

—Straw Weisman, producer, *Pregnant in America*

"Betsy's depth of knowledge, expertise and insights helped our film reach audiences and marketplaces I never knew possible."

—Ward Serrill, filmmaker, *Song of the New Earth*

THE DOCUMENTARY FILMMAKING MASTER CLASS

TELL YOUR STORY FROM CONCEPT TO DISTRIBUTION

BETSY CHASSE

ALLWORTH PRESS
NEW YORK

Allworth Press books may be purchased in bulk at special discounts for sales promotion, corporate gifts, fund-raising, or educational purposes. Special editions can also be created to specifications. For details, contact the Special Sales Department, Allworth Press, 307 West 36th Street, 11th Floor, New York, NY 10018 or info@skyhorsepublishing.com.

23 22 21 20 19   5 4 3 2 1

Published by Allworth Press, an imprint of Skyhorse Publishing, Inc. 307 West 36th Street, 11th Floor, New York, NY 10018. Allworth Press* is a registered trademark of Skyhorse Publishing, Inc.*, a Delaware corporation.

www.allworth.com

Cover design by Mary Belibasakis
Cover photograph by GettyImages/ContentWorks
Author photograph by Betsy Chasse

Library of Congress Cataloging-in-Publication Data
Names: Chasse, Betsy, author.
Title: The documentary filmmaking master class: tell your story from concept
    to distribution / Betsy Chasse.
Description: New York, New York: Allworth Press, an imprint of Skyhorse
    Publishing, [2019] | Includes bibliographical references and index.
Identifiers: LCCN 2019003573 (print) | LCCN 2019010767 (ebook) | ISBN
    9781621537229 (eBook) | ISBN 9781621537212 | ISBN
    9781621537212 (paperback: alk. paper) | ISBN 9781621537229 (ebook)
Subjects: LCSH: Documentary films—Production and direction.
Classification: LCC PN1995.9.D6 (ebook) | LCC PN1995.9.D6 C4368 2019 (print)
    | DDC 070.1/8—dc23
LC record available at https://lccn.loc.gov/2019003573

Print ISBN: 978-1-62153-721-2
eBook ISBN: 978-1-62153-722-9

Printed in the United States of America

> **Regarding all legal documents shared in this book:** All of the legal agreements in this book should be used for reference only. Readers should have all of their agreements reviewed by an attorney who specializes in film, film production, film financing, and investing. Laws change, rules change, and each project is unique and will require specific terms and clauses that may not be reflected in the sample agreements provided here. The author is not a lawyer; she has provided these sample agreements for the reader to begin to gain an understanding of the types of agreements one should have in place. These agreements should not be used without appropriate consultation with an attorney.

Contents

SECTION V: POSTPRODUCTION

SECTION VI: MARKETING AND DISTRIBUTION

SECTION VII: THE WRAP

Introduction

I truly believe everyone has a great story to share, either about their own life journey or that of someone else or something else—be it an event, a discovery, a great journey, or a horrendous crime, whatever it is—something that impacted them in some way. We each have a passion or a desire to tell these stories, and sometimes it isn't just enough to talk about it over coffee or at a dinner party or as a post on social media. We want to have a bigger impact—we want to share it with as many people as possible.

Ever since *Super Size Me* and *What the Bleep Do We Know!?* (both of which opened in theaters around the same time in 2004), the documentary has been making a comeback. With the rise of Netflix, Hulu, Amazon, and many more media outlets clamoring for content, people are grabbing their iPhones and heading out on a journey to make their own films, telling their own stories and maybe hoping to get famous, or to inspire or make an impact, and more important, to not go broke or crazy in the process.

Interestingly, Facebook launched on February 4, 2004, the same day that *What the Bleep Do We Know?!* opened in theaters. I don't think it's mere coincidence that documentaries and reality TV have taken off since then. More people want not only to share real stories, but to hear and watch them. As we have entered an era of "alternative facts," people are looking for information. People are looking for ways to advance their agendas, political views, businesses. YouTube launched in 2005 and became the fastest-growing site on the World Wide Web, averaging more than one million views a day. Clearly there was an audience, and as access to cameras, editing software, and cool tools to make even a novice look even somewhat pro have made it possible for almost anyone to become an internet star.

With the onslaught of content creators came a feeling that quality, storytelling, and filmmaking skill might just disappear. I am happy to say that, at least for me, I see the trend moving back toward quality entertainment, even if the access to distribution and audience has opened up. That's a good thing for people who want to make good films.

The truth is, filmmaking isn't easy. It requires certain skills or the knowledge and ability to hire people who have them. And if you don't have that, the end product suffers greatly. The unfortunate fact is, though there are literally thousands of documentaries on any possible subject, 99 percent of them are just really bad. There is a lot of competition and it's going to take more than an iPhone and a laugh to get more than just your fifteen minutes of viral fame.

Films need to be good in order to break out of the pack and above the noise. It's possible to do this, but it takes more than just talent: it takes some business wisdom and commitment. Whether you're in it to make money, expose something important, share a powerful story, or all of the above, you can make a quality film that reaches your desired audience, impacts them as you hope it will, and do it without going broke, getting lost in the rabbit hole of endless filming and editing, or losing interest altogether and wasting a lot of time and money.

How do you do this? Through planning, organization, clarity, and honest reflection. A lot of filmmaking is learned skills, which is why so many people decide to get a degree in filmmaking. In school, you learn about budgeting, the legalities of filmmaking, how to use a camera, and much more. Most of us don't have the time or the money to go off to film school, and I actually advise most of the young people who ask me to skip it. I tell them to go to business school instead to learn marketing, financing, and law, and in their free time, to get out and start making films themselves: short films, videos, music videos, mini documentaries, or an entire film. The best way to learn filmmaking is by doing it. Unless your desire is to be on the technical side only, i.e., an editor, a cinematographer, a gaffer, etc., then film school probably won't give you anything more than what your own experience and practice can teach you, and nowadays you can take shorter courses to learn the technical aspects of filmmaking.

I don't want to diminish film school. It has its benefits, creating relationships and connections with people who are motivated to make a career in the film industry, access to free equipment and crew, and knowledge and experience. However, with the price tag, I don't recommend going into debt to pay for it.

I hope that by reading this book, you can learn most of what you need without the $50,000 price tag or four years of coursework. In this book, you will learn *process* to follow when you're deciding what documentary to make, how much to spend, how to go about filming it, and how to get it out into the world. For the film student, amateur, or documentary wannabe, this book should be mandatory reading. Frankly, as a film instructor and consultant, I wish I had had a book like this to hand people—a book that covered almost everything they needed to know about the nuts and bolts of preparation and production as well as needed advice about emotional management while making their film.

Making a film is a little like running a country or being a mother. You're creating a world within a world, one that requires a lot of management skills, emotional intelligence, and practical knowledge. You have multiple departments, team leaders, creatives, and technical people all dealing with money and time and, most importantly, helping you share your vision. After more than thirty years in the film business, I'm excited to share everything I know, from deciding on a project to figuring out how to finance it (*Should I apply for that grant or should I ask Uncle Joe for the money? What happens when I spend too much money and Uncle Joe gets mad? How do I make a business plan? Should I say yes to this deal or that one?*). From choosing where it should be distributed to navigating your own emotions and other people's. (Making films can be very stressful!) And on and on . . .

"Art and commerce are not irreconcilable, they are inextricably combined."

—Nicholas Meyer, author and film director,
Star Trek II: The Wrath of Khan and
Star Trek VI: The Undiscovered Country

Too often I find that people embark on the journey of filmmaking without having all the information they need to be successful. They spend more time focusing on their creativity and not enough time focusing on the business. It's important to do both and by doing both, the fact is, you *can* be successful. You can make that impact, tell that story, and enjoy the process, keep your family members and friends, and still eat out once in a while afterward. I am happy to report after thirty years, I'm still standing, thriving, living my life, making the films I want to make, and enjoying the process.

Filmmaking is a craft, an art form, and a business. It requires work on the front end and a lot of work throughout the process. My goal in writing this book is to give you a solid foundation in what you need, how to get it and where to get it from, and some wisdom about the process as well.

BEFORE YOU INVEST YOUR TIME AND MONEY, IS IT WORTH IT?

SECTION I

CHAPTER 1

Questions to Ask Yourself Before You Decide to Embark on This Journey

We all have dreams, ideas, "Aha!" moments in which we leap into the air and, not unlike the Little Rascals, exclaim "Let's put on a show!" I know I do this at least once or twice a week. I meet people every day with Instagram stories, YouTube accounts, aspiring filmmakers and story-tellers who dream of seeing their films on the big screen or going viral.

Usually once the "Great Idea" endorphins wear off, we tell our-selves that while it sounded great then, it may not be so practical now. But sometimes that doesn't happen. Sometimes the idea sticks with you for days, weeks, even months, and you can't seem to shake the desire to get it out of your head and into the world. If that's happening to you now, then that's the first step in deciding whether or not you want to embark on a journey to make a film.

Deciding to make a documentary is a huge decision. Films can be costly, not only in money, but also in time and emotional health. I'm not talking about heading out for a weekend of fun with your friends and seeing what happens. I'm talking about undertaking a huge proj-ect. A film, a docuseries, a web series. A project that surely takes time, money, and effort.

Before making this decision, you need to ask yourself a few ques-tions: *Why is this documentary needed? What is my intention with this documentary? Do I have the time and energy to fully commit to making it? What is the outcome I desire from making it?*

These questions are paramount to your being successful. Skipping them or skimping on them will only lead to disappointment later. Trust me, I've been there. I have met with too many filmmakers who jumped in and regretted it later. Commitment and expectations are two of the most important issues we tend to try to avoid examining thoroughly. We make a lot of assumptions around these words, and I can tell you from firsthand experience that not having conversations about what they mean to you (and your partners, crew, and anyone else involved in your film) will result in a lot of bruised egos, upset, and sometimes an unfinished project. So don't be afraid to have the hard conversations, especially at the beginning when you haven't risked your time, money (yours or someone else's), and your emotional well-being.

What is your level of commitment? What does that word mean to you? Are you all-in no matter what or are you dipping your toe in the water? What about those who are joining you on this adventure? What are your expectations of yourself and your partners?

Having this conversation openly and honestly will save you a lot of stress, disappointment, and even relationships later on. Give yourself and everyone you discuss this with permission to hesitate, to think about it. It's better you know *now* where everyone is at than when it's too late.

I won't sugarcoat it. Making a film, any film, is hard. It's a lot like having a baby and raising it. It's unpredictable, costly, frustrating, infuriating; it can make you feel so amazingly high and bring you to your knees. Just ask anyone who's done it. . . .

Here are a couple sample comments from friends who are filmmakers:

> "Filmmaking has been, for me, the most rewarding and soul crushing experience of my life."
> —Ben Fama Jr., filmmaker,
> *A Virus Called Fear* and *A Reason to Believe*

> "I never thought you could love something and hate something simultaneously."
> —Katheryne Thomas, filmmaker, *The Principle*

And a couple from really famous filmmakers:

> "Filmmaking is a chance to live many lifetimes."
>
> —Robert Altman, Academy
> Award–winning director, *MASH*

> "Filmmaking can give you everything, but at the same time, it can take everything from you."
>
> —Alejandro González Iñárritu,
> Academy Award–winning filmmaker, *Birdman*

I promise I'm not telling you this to talk you out of it or to scare you. (OK, maybe a little). I'm sharing this with you because if you're going to make a film, then you have to be prepared to bleed for it, live for it, die for it. Well, maybe that's a bit dramatic. But you get my drift.

First and foremost, filmmaking is art. Storytelling is an art form, and even if you're making a biopic about the guy who invented the straw, unless you reach into your audience's hearts and touch them, it won't have the impact you're hoping for. If you don't have the passion for it, then your film won't have the passion in it. So you have to be committed, even when it's hard and it feels like it's not going to happen or work out. (And that is going to happen, at least once.)

So be sure you're committed. And if you aren't right now, that's OK. You may be later on. Or maybe you never will be. You may not know yet. Finish this book, ask yourself all the questions in this chapter, sit with them, write in your journal about them, and make sure your answers fully resonate with you.

The next question for you to ponder: *Is this documentary needed?*

They say there are no new stories, that every story has been told, and I find that to be true. In the world of documentaries, there are only so many films that can be made about the guy who invented the straw and find a home. Do some research, check out what's out there. Has the story been told your way? Can you add anything to the conversation? Is there something unique you can add or share?

Just because a story has been told doesn't mean you can't tell it again. The key is to find your own voice, your own version, and to differentiate yourself from anyone else who might be out there. If that idea isn't in your head yet, then chances are you should stop your journey until that idea has come.

Watch the other films about your topic. Some people will tell you not to do this, lest those other ideas contaminate your own. I personally disagree with this notion. However, you need to decide for yourself. I find watching other films, other documentaries, helps me define my own style and what I want to say. Later in this book we're going to explore the six modes of documentary films—Poetic, Expository, Observational, Participatory, Reflexive, and Performative—and what each style means, how to use them, and when to use them. Nowadays, I enjoy seeing how documentaries mix these styles. By watching other films, you'll get a sense for what you like and what your film needs in order to tell its story. In the next few chapters, we will explore in more detail how to do your research so it's effective and helpful and doesn't impede your progress and your own vision.

Talk to other filmmakers. Ask them to share their successes and their failures. What worked for them and what didn't? Now is the time, before you're too far in it to take notes and listen to others share their wisdom.

Read the trades. There are tons of great websites and trade magazines with wonderful articles written by people who have been there and done that. Their experience might be unique, but knowledge is power. Some suggestions I like: *Documentary Magazine, Filmmaker Magazine, IndieWire, MovieMaker.*

Why do you want to make this film? What's your agenda? Look, we all have an agenda. To be able to clearly identify yours early on in the process will allow you to be a better decision maker in all aspects of your film. Being honest about *your* reason why will help you become a better filmmaker.

I want to change the world.

I want to change policy.

I want to inform people about a story that impacted me.

I want to inspire people.

I want to make money...

It's OK to say you want to make money. This seems to be a hard truth for documentary filmmakers to utter. Mostly they want to seem like they have some altruistic reason around making the world a better place. Both can actually be possible. Or maybe it's truly for a noble cause and you have no need to profit from it or to be paid. It doesn't matter. What matters is you know your why and what your expectations are around making the film and what you hope to get out of it. Do you want to change the world or a part of it? Do you want to expose some hidden truth? Do you want to share some great piece of wisdom? Do you want to shed light on a part of the world that needs it? Write this down, get clarity around it. Own it.

Not only will this empower you as a filmmaker, but it will also help you when you're creating your business plan and when you're looking to secure funding. People will want to know the reasons you're making this film, whether it's when you're asking them for money or for their time. Eventually, even your audience will want to know your inspiration. I like to write this down on a card and put it in my workspace. It helps me when I'm having a moment of confusion or questioning what my next steps are or what decision I should make. I examine each possible decision and then I ask, *Which one fits my why? Which decision fits my agenda?* If a decision is out of alignment with your why, then it's a no; if it fits, then it's a yes. When you have clarity on your why, decision making becomes much less stressful and you become a better leader too. People respect you because they see you are acting in alignment with your stated goals and in alignment with what is best for the project.

What is the outcome you want from making the film? This is slightly different than your why in that this is really about impact and how that impact will be made. You could say, "I want to make this film because I want to shed light on the amazing story of one man's journey to invent something unique and unusual, his trials and triumphs, and how he never gave up. By making this film, I want to inspire others to never give up." Or you could say, "I want to change people's worldview" or "I want to change policy" All of these whys will help your film be better and your statements be clearer. They will also guide you when you're creating your marketing plan and possibly other products, books, educational materials, etc.

What would this outcome look like? In the real world, how does that outcome manifest itself? Is it a course people take? Is it a nonprofit that gets shared? Is it hordes of happy filmgoers walking out of the theater crying with inspired tears? What do you want to see when people leave the theater?

This answer, along with your why, will become your mission statement or agenda. Your mission statement isn't about *your* why alone: it is about the "universal" why or the collective why. Writing a mission statement will help you, especially in your creative process. In the editing room, it will help you choose between takes and decide when to cut to another shot and when to let it hold. It will help you with your budget. You can ask yourself, *Will spending this money add to the overall production value I desire for my film? Will filming this piece get me the outcome I want from my audience?* Write down your agenda on your card next to your why. When something comes up, hold the issue up against your mission statement, and your decision will be clear.

Creating a film isn't all about the nuts and bolts and the logistics of it all. Film is emotional, it's psychological—not only for the viewer, but also for the creator and everyone involved in the making of a film. Becoming aware of yourself, of your own beliefs about the film, about your ego needs and agendas, connecting to your intuition . . . to me, these things are far more important to know about than a new piece of editing software. Technology is easy, trust me! There's always a video on YouTube you can watch. What's far harder and far more intricate and far more important is dealing with the psychology of producing a film.

Listen, there's nothing bad about having an ego. The reality is, we all have an ego, and most people embarking on a journey like this, people with a desire to make an impact on the world, have a big one.

The trick is to learn to tell the difference between when your ego wants to be cool and when your ego wants the film to have an impact and help change the world.

So how do you get there? How do you differentiate agendas? How do you empower the film and not just yourself?

I wrestle with this issue with every film I make. And here is what I do every time: *I give the project independence.* I give it its own ego and sense of self. Why? Because if I don't, then I'm liable to get caught up in my own why, my own desire to be right and to be in control, which means I close off all opportunity for collaboration. This might seem confusing because I asked you *your* why, *your* agenda. However, if you really took the time to think about it, you were essentially channeling your film and *its* why and *its* agenda. You are simply the messenger: the conduit for this message to be seen and heard.

> "A film is never really good unless the camera is an eye in the head of a poet."
>
> —Orson Welles

Don't let that quote discourage you. Not everyone is a poet. But it's important that no matter what your subject is, you tell a story, not only factually, informationally, but emotionally.

Films are essentially pieces of collaborative art. Your project may be your vision, but eventually your vision will be interpreted by others on your team. When you can identify your film's why—its mission and purpose—from the perspective of the film as a whole instead of it just being about you, a lot of potential is opened up for great ideas from other places—other producers, crew, interview subjects—from anywhere. This is part of what we'll discuss when we talk about hiring your crew and choosing who you interview and how you prepare. We have a tendency to want to project our agenda and ourselves into the story and in doing so we don't listen very well. One of the best assets you can have as a leader, an interviewer, and a filmmaker is being a good listener.

So you've already laid out your agenda and your why. Now, just to be sure, ask the *film* if they are aligned. Check in with your gut, often, to make sure it's on the path it should be. You'll know this when it is. It will feel right, someone will say something that will inspire something within you and the direction, the decision, the choice will be clear.

> "Intuition is the key to everything, in painting, filmmaking, business—everything. I think you could have an intellectual ability, but if you can sharpen your intuition, which they say is emotion and intellect joining together, then a knowingness occurs."
>
> —David Lynch

I'm talking about learning to trust your intuition. It will save you every time.

Having the ability to truly *listen* to your intuition and listen to others is one of the most powerful tools you have as a filmmaker. This isn't some woo-woo New Age concept. Read about many of your favorite filmmakers and how they approach a film, and many of them will say that the film is an entity all its own and that they are simply the conduit for the message. Even if you're a lone wolf, filming yourself, editing yourself, doing it all, being open to allowing the film to have its own voice, to speak up when something isn't right or to resonate when it is, will allow you to tell the story that needs to be told, the story that, right now, is taking up all your free space in your heart and mind. It's hard to trust your gut or follow your intuition when you're doing something new or unknown to you. This is why taking time before you start to create a plan, do your research, and have the honest conversations with yourself about what you're willing to do, spend, and give up or not is key, and when you do that, you've created a foundation for a very good relationship with your intuition.

Ask your film, "Why me?" Why should you be the one to make this film, giving up your valuable time, assets, and energy? What will happen if you don't make this film? How will you feel if you don't make it? How will you feel if it fails?

The answers to these questions don't have to be perfect or pretty. They don't have to all be rah-rah either. You just have to know what they are, for you, right now. Some of the answers may change as time goes by, some won't. I have this conversation with myself often as I'm in the midst of a project.

I spend a lot of time dreaming about the possibilities, thinking through what could happen, all the possible scenarios. This might seem like I'm overthinking. Right now, before you've become invested in the project, is the best time to do this. Now is the time to really examine how you will feel if it doesn't turn out the way you want it to and how will you feel if you don't get that interview, to consider what are the other options available to you. What are plans A, B, and C (and even D, E, and F)? Write them out; budget them out. Filmmaking is like a great maze: there are endless possibilities, so have a few ready to go, and when the shit hits the fan, you'll have a baby wipe at the ready and you can wipe your face and keep on moving.

Well, here you are. You've taken the most important step. You've done some soul-searching, you've come to some clarity about why you want to make this film and why this film wants you to make it. So, before we move on, let's first have a short conversation about failure.

Most films fail, and by that, I mean that most films never live up to the hopes and dreams of those who made them. They don't make money, they don't get distribution, etc., and yet most filmmakers look back on their failures with awe and gratitude. I know I have. The truth is, if you do your homework, plan thoroughly, have the tough conversations, and answer honestly and listen with integrity, you'll have gained so much even if your film epically fails. Filmmaking, for me, has been a great teacher. Not only that, but it's been a great adventure, one worth embarking on!

The good news is that it's also true that most finished films, unless they are just utterly horrible, usually find some kind of audience. Just think of Tommy Wiseau's *The Room*, considered the worst movie ever.

Eventually, a memoir about Tommy's making of the film was turned into *The Disaster Artist*, directed by and starring James Franco and nominated for an Academy Award.[1] Even today as I write this, *The Room* is still playing in local art houses, having gone from disaster to pop culture hit. . . .

If you can't stop dreaming about your film, can't let go of the idea and will literally die if you don't make it, then go for it. Why not? What else are you going to do? You don't want to be at the end of your life wishing you had done it. This is what life is for, and with the right tools, research, and practical knowledge, you will probably have the time of your life. Have fun. Enjoy it, even when it sucks—and it will sometimes. No great adventure is an adventure without going through a bit of the dark night of the soul. What a great gift to be able to tell a story, to explore an idea into its deepest core, to get into the soul of a dream that wants to emerge. No matter what, you've brought it out into this reality, and in doing that you have already succeeded.

---

1   Kirsten Chuba, "'The Disaster Artist': 10 of the Film's Stars and Their Real-Life Inspirations," *Hollywood Reporter*, December 1, 2017, https://www.hollywoodreporter.com/lists/true-story-disaster-artist-how-accurate-are-characters-1047099.

CHAPTER 2

A Little Research Goes a Long Way

OK, you've committed to making your film, you know your why and what you want to accomplish. You're ready for the next step. Now you need to be realistic and discover if it's *needed*. Who might watch it? Why will they watch it? Has the topic already been covered? If so, what new slant can you take on the subject? All of this research comes in handy when you create your business plan (even if you intend to fund it yourself, make a business plan!), and of course when you're outlining and scripting your film. Knowing as much as you can about not only your subject matter but also the business of documentary filmmaking will set the foundation for a successful project.

I follow a very simple plan when doing research. As you can see I love my Ws: Who, What, When, Where, and Why.

WHO

Who is this movie for? If your answer is "Everybody will love my movie!" then you haven't done your research. No, not everyone will love your movie. It's important to understand two aspects of your *who:*

1. **Demographics:** This is more statistical information about who would love your movie. Consider age, gender, income, education, location, ethnicity, and so forth.

2. **Psychographics:** This is more about the psychology of who would love your movie—their *why*, so to speak. These are subgroups based on philosophy, ideology, and beliefs rather than income and education.

Why do you need both? Because there are often 50-year-old skateboarders out there and if you simply focused on the demographics, you'd be missing a huge chunk of your audience. People are multifaceted and have varying interests. Getting to know your viewer will not only help you market to them when the film is finished, but it will also help you make decisions during production. In these modern times, the use of psychographics is what enables Facebook and Google to send you ads simply because you thought about buying mint chip ice cream.

If you want to understand marketing, research the father of PR and propaganda, Edward Bernays. He is most famous for creating the campaign to encourage women to smoke. He knew the power of understanding the psychographics of his audience and how to use it.

For many, marketing is that evil, but if you want your film to be seen, it's time to embrace it. Use these powers for good! I'm going to assume that your desire is to make a quality film, one that informs, inspires, and is honest and truthful, that you aren't going to make a film that causes harm. . . . I have no guarantees, but I am an eternal optimist.

Google has made research much easier and a lot less expensive than when you had to purchase market research, so become a Google ninja and start looking into your audience, their spending habits, where they go to learn or experience the topic of your film. For example, how many books have they read on the subject? Are there conferences, large events, other films, etc., about it? (FYI: The other films will be important when you prepare your business plan because you will use them as comparables—so find out as much as you can about their budgets, the revenues, and how many markets are they available in.)

What is the market share for your film's topic? As in, how many people are interested in it, how much money do they spend on it each year? Google statistics. These will come in handy while preparing your business plan. If two million people in the US are affected by a specific disease you are exploring in your documentary, then that will give you an idea of how many potential viewers you have. In addition to those affected, consider their family members and other people impacted by their situation. Is there a nonprofit or several that focus on your topic?

I often call up those filmmakers, companies, or people who have created products and services around my topic. Most of them will talk with you, some of them will give you their budgets and revenues, and some won't. It's also a great way to find subjects to interview or possible events to film for B-roll.[2] Don't worry about anyone stealing your idea; that doesn't happen as often as people think, and if someone does, well, you have recourse.

Talk to people who might be interested in your film and ask them what they would like to see or learn. Who would they want to interview if they could? It's time to get up close and personal with your audience.

The point is to know your audience like you know your best friend (their spending habits, their social media habits) and gauge their level of interest. How much will they spend to see your movie? How far will they travel? Are they more likely to see it in a movie theater or online, or via pay cable or on Netflix?

Not only will this help you make a better film, but it will also help you market the film and hopefully achieve your goal of paying off your investors (if you have them) and getting your film seen by as many people as possible. I suspect you're not making a film just so your mom and Uncle Joe can watch it in your living room. This doesn't have to impede your vision for your film. It will enhance it.

---

2   B-roll is footage often layered with voice-over, commonly used for transitioning between scenes or providing details. Examples may include: establishing shots of the location (city, landscape, etc.), action shots of the subjects (people performing tasks, animals migrating, etc.), and close-up shots (hands working, machinery functioning, etc.).

WHAT

What is it you're actually making? You might say "I'm making a documentary!" but maybe you shouldn't. Documentaries don't sound sexy and fun, and most of them usually don't make any money. A lot of them end up at the bottom of the Netflix list, hoping some late-night binger is desperate for something to watch. I'm not trying to discourage you—it's just important to be realistic and clear about what format your project should end up in.

Maybe your feature-length documentary would do better as a docuseries or a web series. I love this format and have used it multiple times. It offers more opportunity to explore the subject in depth and more avenues for distribution. You can create one-hour, half-hour, or even 15-minute episodes. You can film a few and use those to generate further funding.

Maybe your feature-length documentary is really a one-hour documentary or even a short documentary? This is a wonderful way to maximize a smaller budget or to explore a topic that already has been covered in other formats but you have something new to add. Again, you can still sell short documentaries to Netflix, Amazon Prime, or even Vimeo! Short documentaries are great when there is a narrative feature about the same subject. Create a strategic partnership to share the short doc with the narrative feature to further the distribution!

Sometimes this isn't figured out until after you're done filming. It is often said that a film is made at least three times: once in your head, once while filming, and once in the editing room. Often it may not even look like the film you envisioned when you started. But you may be able to figure this out before you start filming, which is ideal. It will of course determine your budget, shooting schedule, and how to seek funding.

Don't be attached to making a feature-length documentary. Let your story decide. It's also important to consider your audience. If your audience is young and doesn't usually spend money on going to a movie unless it's a blockbuster, then perhaps looking at other formats will generate better opportunities for your film to be seen.

Remember your goals and your why. This will help you decide what format your film should end up in.

WHEN

When do you need to have your documentary finished? Are you going for a festival run? Does it need to be timed to a specific event? All of the above? How long will it take you to produce it? This is important because timing is everything.

As an example—this is why research is key—I was asked to come on board a documentary that had been filming for two years but was stuck in the edit bay. The first question I asked the filmmaker (after asking how much they'd spent) was if any other events, films, books, etc., were out or coming out that might be competitive. They hadn't really researched that. As it turns out, there was another film: exact same subject matter and coming out in six months, only with a celebrity at the helm. We were able to get a sneak peek at that film and then rework our cut. While our subject matter was the same, we had a completely unique take on the subject, and we used the promotion from the *other* film as a catalyst for our own distribution. We piggybacked on the success of that film. We didn't get a theatrical release, but we were able to make deals because that film was successful, and our film had a different perspective. Competition or comparable projects don't have to be the curse of death. Especially when you're prepared.

It's not easy to find out what other projects are out there, but by networking, checking out film festivals, and searching on IMDb, you can get a lot of information about what projects are coming and what their status is, i.e., development, preproduction, production, postproduction.

Research what film festivals might fit your film, or where your film has a likely chance of being accepted, and when their submission deadlines are. Also look into what events are coming up that might tie in with your release. Doing that can give you a good idea of when the right time is to have your film ready. As an example, February is Black History Month. If your theme is related, should you schedule your release to coincide with that celebration? Each month usually has at least one national-awareness theme, and those can be used to generate media attention and buzz about your film.

WHERE

Everybody has a dream of watching their film on the big screen. Sadly, especially nowadays, theatrical distribution is often out of reach and usually not worth it. When I begin to plan my projects, I usually have a theatrical plan as well as a digital-release plan. When the film is finished, I'm ready for either to move forward. It's possible to do a small theatrical release if your desire is to be considered for awards. You can do this on your own or work with companies that do Academy-eligible releases.[3] (This can get very expensive—plan for at least $25,000 to $30,000.)

Most documentaries start their "where" journey in film festivals. I'll explore film festivals in more detail in Chapter 16. For research, you should look at which film festivals are looking for films like yours and which film festivals have generated success for past documentaries. You don't have to enter every film festival; it's cost prohibitive and ultimately doesn't really help your film. I've seen films with more than a hundred film-festival wins waste away, and films with zero wins hit the theaters.

As I mentioned above, your audience will have a big impact on your where. It's said that about 60 percent of all media content is viewed on a phone or other handheld device. This is important not only because it will impact the way you shoot your film, but also where you distribute it. The number of platforms available and looking for content has tripled in the last three years, and it doesn't seem to be slowing down. Everybody wants to land either in a theater or on Netflix or HBO, but don't discount newer, smaller platforms that might do more for your film. ESPN, NFL, Animal Planet, Pop TV—they are all looking for content.

---

3   The Academy has specific guidelines in order to be considered for an award, depending on the category. These companies will make sure you meet the guidelines.

Once you've finished your pitch deck, sizzle reel, and business plan (all explained in Chapter 6), you can start setting up meetings with development executives, sales agents, producers' reps.

How do you connect with those people? Networking, networking, networking. It's all about who you know, so start getting to know people. Join meet-ups, business groups, the International Documentary Association (IDA), and start going to events, talks, conferences. Begin creating relationships with people who can connect the dots when you need them.

This part of the business of film is not for those who are introverts. If you are more inclined to hide behind the camera or in the editing room, hire a good producer. You're going to need every one of those contacts at some point along your filmmaking journey, so start making them as early as possible.

WHY

You've done your why, so now it's time to ask: Why this documentary *now*? This is the easiest question to answer if you've answered all the other Ws. You should see a need for your film and you should see that there is enough interest in your film for it to generate revenue, that people will pay for it or even watch it. You should be able to gauge how much it's worth, how much you should spend on it, and where it will most likely land once it's done.

All of this information will guide you as you move forward. This will help you determine your budget, time spent, and expectations in terms of outcome. It will give you wisdom on what possible issues may come up, potholes along the road to watch out for. You will learn from other people's mistakes and what worked for them. There is nothing wrong with taking what worked from others and learning from what didn't.

We often like to spend time researching our subject and less time researching the business side of our film. Don't skimp here. Not only will this save you time and money, but it will make your film better.

In order to regroup on one of my documentaries, when another film beat us to the theaters, we had to film more and take more time editing. Had they done their homework beforehand, we probably could have released earlier and been the theatrical. It worked out in the end, but it cost a whole lot more.

CHAPTER 3

What Is It Worth to You and the World?

The multimillion-dollar question of every film project is: how much is it going to cost vs. how much is it going to make?! People often approach this backward. The truth is, a film can cost anywhere from $100 to more than a $100 million. Ultimately it depends on how much money you have and are willing to risk. You should only spend what you can, and you should spend less than what you think you'll profit. That raises a new question: Do you need to make money from this film? Are you planning on getting investors? Grants? Loans? Crowdfunding?

In Section III, I will go into detail about how to crowdfund, apply for grants, and seek investors. But before you do any of that, you need to determine how much to spend on your project.

The easy answer is: as little as possible but as much as you can to fully express your vision.

The reality is that good films cost money. For sure you can get people to work for free, you can do it all yourself, and you can make a film for no money at all. And that's really hard. Honestly, I don't recommend the lone-wolf approach to filmmaking. Having people work for free opens up a whole new discussion around commitment and expectations. The old saying "You get what you pay for" often rings true in this scenario, and if you're willing to put all this effort into making a film, taking time to raise some money to pay for it is worth the effort. It's not as difficult as you might think, and it's actually much easier to raise a little money than it is to make a film for absolutely nothing.

Even if you plan to do it all for nothing, having a realistic budget will help you see what you really need to make the film you want and hopefully stop you from wasting time and money on stuff you don't need.

Here's a funny thing about making it for free: it never is. You've got to eat or feed people; you've got to buy gas to get to the location; you're going to need some equipment, tape, paper, pens, cell phone service, software, etc. You're going to need to pay for stuff, so be honest: it's not free.

Looking at your comparables (other films similar in market and genre to your own), knowing what they spent vs. what revenues they generated is a good place to start. Did they spend too much? Not enough? Using their numbers will help you determine a realistic budget. It's important to consider not only the production budget, but also the marketing budget. This isn't easy information to find. By looking at how they marketed (e.g., social media ads, radio, TV, print?) their film, you can generally figure out how much they spent. Include in your budget both production and marketing expenses. Researching what Netflix, Hulu, pay-cable channels, etc. are currently paying for documentaries will help you determine your budget. Can you sell it worldwide? Consider all markets when running your comparables. Don't be shy! Pick up the phone and ask questions.

TIP: You can usually find the distributor of any film in the credits, domestic and/or foreign, and it's also listed on IMDbPro. Pick up the phone and call them. Visit American Film Market (AFM) and see what documentaries are being marketed there. I could provide you with a list of distributors, but unfortunately it would probably be out of date as I finished typing it. Companies come and go. Google documentary-distribution platforms, and check out the most recent articles and lists. The IDA often has updated lists and events where you can meet distributors as well as other filmmakers. It's worth it to become a member for their resources.

Finding out how much people spent on their films and what they actually made is probably the hardest research you're going to do. It's also the most important. How much you spend—and how you spend it—will directly affect the success of your film.

Now is the time to talk to as many collaborators (directors of photography, or DPs; editors; animators; etc.) as you can and get multiple bids to determine what it's going to cost to get your vision out of your head and onto the screen.

When you were examining your why, I asked if you needed to make money off this film. It's OK to want to make money! I'm surprised how often people shy away from being honest about this question. If you have an investor (even if it's your family), at least recouping their investment will go a long way in being able to call your film a success. Plus, if you're inclined to make another one, it will give you a track record to show. Most people I've met who have made one film usually want to make more. It can be that addictive! Is this a passion project you're willing to go broke on? Even if it is, setting up a specified budget will help you plan and organize and avoid regret later on. No one wants to lose money, and even if your desire is just to share a great story and you're not worried about getting your money back, know that it's possible to do both and actually much more rewarding that way.

Is this project a marketing tool for something else? Often people will make a short or even feature-length documentary that is used to drive people to a specific product or service. Have you run the potential revenue streams from that product or service? Your marketing budget for that will determine how much you spend on your film.

A great example of this is well.org. They make film after film to drive people to their website, where they sell products, services, and courses all related to the topics of their films. They give their movies away for free; all you have to do is join their e-mail list (building their platform), and then they send you targeted e-mails based on the film you have watched, which sells their products. Pretty smart, actually. Their budgets reflect their expected ROI (return on investment) on whatever product or products they are selling. It's a marketing expense. Films make incredible marketing tools. Look at most major brands: they are all using stories as a way to market their products.

If you are planning on getting an investor, then you will need to be able to provide a budget, including marketing and distribution (film festival costs, delivery elements), as well as an ROI. Your budget should be at least 25 percent below your expected ROI so your investors can see that they will not only make their money back, but also make some money for their risk. When creating an ROI, always, always, always use the word *estimated* before "Return on Investment." You do not want to make promises you can't keep, especially around profit margins.

Much of this (the 25 percent below ROI, the comparables, even your budget) are best guesses. Good research will get you close, but probably not 100 percent right. It took me years as a production manager and line producer to really be able to accurately predict what a film would cost. Especially now, while you're still in the planning stages, budget higher than you expect and calculate your ROI conservatively. This should help you find the balance. Be realistic now and cut corners later. Gas, food, and lodging are things people often forget to budget for; taxes (your LLC filing), office supplies, and monthly costs (like web hosting) also seem to be forgotten easily. Remember, your film is a business that will live on (hopefully) for years after you make it.

I always recommend starting a separate LLC for each project. This protects you from any lawsuits or injunctions that might arise. Consult with your CPA and attorney on what is best for you and your financial situation. If you enter into any profit-sharing agreement, having an LLC will become absolutely necessary.

I'll say this often. Your film is not just your creative expression. It's a business transaction. Treat it like one. Protect yourself and your assets. Be smart and work with people who understand the nuances of the film industry, legally and financially.

As a final thought, I typically would not spend more than $200,000 to $300,000 on a documentary. I would even go as far as to say you should not spend more than $50,000, especially if this is your first go at it and you don't have a guaranteed ROI (in terms of presales or a guaranteed distribution deal). Regardless of all the pumped-up headlines you'll find about how documentaries are a huge source of revenues for places like Netflix, etc., typically for the filmmaker, they aren't. And unless you've got an Academy Award or a celebrity on board or own the rights to a very hot topic, it's not likely you'll get much out of the big names, and after you consider the cost of marketing and distribution and what people are actually willing to pay, you'll realize that recouping is extremely difficult.

Most of us make documentaries out of passion for the subject matter and are grateful if it somehow supports us along the way.

THE BUSINESS PLAN

CHAPTER 4

What Is a Business Plan and Why Do I Need It?

It sounds obvious. Everybody has a business plan for their project, right? Sadly, many people get gung-ho to get started and then realize they are in over their head.

A business plan serves a couple of purposes:

1. If you're seeking any type of investment, you'll need one to provide to potential investors.
2. It's a road map for you to follow. Often filmmakers get excited and passionate and end up taking a detour, but a business plan can help you stay on track and know when you need to stick to the map and when it's OK to veer off a bit.

A business plan is more than a pitch deck. A pitch deck is a fancy pdf or PowerPoint presentation (often people create websites) with a synopsis, some images, and bullet points about how successful your film is going to be, the market, and basics about the marketing strategy—all the good stuff. It's what you use to get people interested in your project. This is a short bullet-point version of your more detailed business plan.

It's OK in the pitch deck to be your own cheerleader. This document is meant to excite the reader/viewer. Make it visual. Have your artwork/poster/logo designed. (This can change later if need be.) Remember, you are pitching a visual project, so make your deck visual yet classy. There is a balance to this, and sometimes people can go overboard with the art and lose viewers by not having just enough information to make want them to ask for the full plan.

Even if you're self-funding or Uncle Joe is giving you the money (and especially if the money is coming from someone else), create a business plan. Trust me: when family is involved, you must provide a business plan and have a contract. There is nothing more destructive to a family relationship than money lost or money owed. Most projects that make it to the finish line got there because they started with a plan that had a beginning, a middle and an end, just like your film needs to have. I've seen too many filmmakers lost in the weeds, three years in with too much footage and no idea how to finish, simply because they didn't have a plan.

PICKING YOUR DOCUMENTARY STYLE

One of the most important aspects of your plan (and expressing your vision) is the style of your documentary and your ability to explain it. What is your storytelling style? This will guide you in every aspect of your project, such as who you interview and how you film those interviews, plus your music, lighting, visuals, and marketing materials. I hope you've spent time watching tons and tons of documentaries, focusing in on what you like and don't like and listening for what style will best suit your topic.

As I've mentioned before, what's going to get you the deal, especially when pitching studios or investors and even when crowdfunding, is not only your planning, but also your ability to clearly express the story you want to make and how you intend to make it.

Some people like to create a look book in addition to their pitch deck. They can be especially helpful if you are pitching your documentary in person. You can create a digital look book or an old-fashioned printed portfolio. The look book might have color schemes, location looks, shot looks, a storyboard of an animated sequence, or examples of graphics—anything visual to show anyone you are pitching that you have a vision. It's also helpful as a director to have these references for your crew and for yourself.

In an interview on an episode of KCRW's *The Business*, Lisa Nishimura, head of Netflix's original documentary and comedy programming, was asked how she chose one documentary over the other.[4] Having a compelling story and a unique perspective or POV was important, of course; but besides that, she said it was the filmmaker's passion for the subject matter and the ability to express it (i.e., clarity about your film). She wants to know: What's your vision? Why should *you* be the one to make this film? (All those big questions I asked you to get clarity on in the beginning of this book.) Most importantly, what sets your film apart and makes it worthy of being Netflix-original programming?

Documentaries are entertainment: never forget that, Even though they are also designed to inform and inspire, they are stories that need to be compelling, visually interesting, emotionally expressive, and experiential for the viewer.

Documentary film began with the Lumière Brothers, inventors of a combination movie camera and projector. They began by filming real events, but one would be hard-pressed to call those documentaries; they were more like camera tests. It really wasn't until the 1920s that people got the idea to make narrative documentaries, the first two popular docs being *Man with a Movie Camera* (1929) and *Nanook of the North* (1922). Each are different in their approach to style and form. Alice Guy, who was a secretary for the Lumière Brothers, is credited with the first narrative film, *La Fée aux Choux* (*The Cabbage Patch Fairy*); she went on to become considered the "mother of cinema."

From there, people were in a truly experimental phase of all forms of documentary and storytelling. *War of the Worlds* (1938), although a radio show, played deeply into the idea of reality—what is real and what is fiction.

Eventually documentaries became a useful tool for disseminating information, an idea, or an ideology. Propaganda was born, and the

---

4   Kim Masters, "Lisa Nishimura on How She Picks Documentaries for Netflix," KCRW, podcast recording, 6:34, December 10, 2018, https://www.kcrw.com/culture/shows/the-business/kristoffer-polaha-on-hallmark-movies-netflixs-lisa-nishimura/lisa-nishimura-on-how-she-picks-documentaries-for-netflix

documentary format suited this need very well. Adolf Hitler loved the documentary format, as did the propagandists hired to write and proliferate different agendas worldwide.

For a while after the 1950s and 1960s, documentary took on a decidedly high-brow approach to facts and fiction and became mostly newsy in style and delivery. Documentary filmmakers became purists, and with the rise in popularity of television, documentary became journalism.

Ironically, my film *What the Bleep Do We Know?!* was disqualified from the documentary category at the Academy Awards because we had too many fictional scenes, even though those scenes were simply a visual representation or "reenactment" of what our experts had said. For a while, this was considered a no-no in documentary filmmaking. Just the facts, ma'am, and leave out the reenactments or fictional explanations.

What blew this notion wide-open were two things, at least in my opinion: reality TV and films like *The Imposter,* which is absolutely a must-watch. Documentaries came full circle and embraced an "old" approach to embodying the many forms of storytelling in a new way. Today, you can't turn on an episode of *Expedition Unknown* with Josh Gates without a reenactment of some event in history.

There are basically six modes of documentaries. Some filmmakers stick strictly to one mode, but more often people mix and match styles to suit their topic. These modes were developed by Bill Nichols, an American documentary theorist.

An assignment I gave all my students regardless of their skills in editing and cinematography, the two biggest hurdles to going it alone, was to pick a style and make a short one- to three-minute piece using one specific mode. This can help you find your style, and as a side benefit it will help you become familiar with the two other most important jobs on your set. All jobs are important, from production assistant to producer, but understanding how to communicate your vision to other creatives is paramount to having your vision manifest on the screen. Learning a little bit about cinematography and editing will help you immensely in your communication. I understand a lot about both and am terrible at executing both.

Have some fun with your iPhone and iMovie, if nothing else. Do a test interview and practice editing it with B-roll. Choose a song and make a music video. I actually accomplish a lot with iMovie. You can also purchase a monthly subscription to Adobe, and there are tons of how-to videos on YouTube for any editing program.

Here's a quick tip. Learn the basics of whatever program your editor will be using (it's probably either Adobe Premiere Pro or Final Cut Pro). This way, when you get your footage, you can pull and bin the pieces you like and assemble them in an order you like. This will help with the editing process. I always have my footage transcribed immediately after I film it. Some filmmakers do this themselves; I don't. This is one of those scenarios where it is "better to pay someone who's fast at it" than to wait. I use people on Fiverr and rev.com, both reasonably priced and quick. (Make sure to ask them to list time code every two minutes.) Then I read everything, mark what I like, jump on whatever platform is being used by my editor, pull my pieces, bin them, and send them to the editor!

WHAT ARE THE SIX DIFFERENT MODES OF DOCUMENTARIES?

Poetic Mode

Think music video with a story. Not a lot of dialogue, or maybe none at all, musical and visual. More inclined to express a mood or a tone rather than follow a linear script. *Koyaanisqatsi* by Godfrey Reggio is a good example. I use this mode when I'm telling a story through emotions and feeling that's less focused on a linear timeline with lots of facts. A great way to practice this mode is to choose a piece of music you love and pair it with visuals, allowing the music to be your guide. You can either tell a story with the visuals or simply move from one image to the other, allowing the viewers to fill in the story with how they feel.

Expository Mode

If the Poetic Mode is more about showing and allowing the viewer to feel through music and visuals, the Expository Mode is all about telling. It's about giving information, using a narrator as the "voice of God" or an expert providing informed rhetoric over lots of B-roll to visually explain what is being said in voice-over. Just watch *Dateline NBC* or *60 Minutes* or any longer news piece as an example of Expository Mode. A great way to practice this mode is to interview someone telling you a story about an event moment by moment, and then intercut that interview with visuals and using the interview subject as voice-over, adding in a narrator to fill in gaps in facts and story, ask questions, and lead the viewer to your conclusion. This mode is likely going to drive the viewer to a specific outcome or opinion, probably the same opinion you, the filmmaker has, but not always. There have been expository documentaries that have no outcome—the killer wasn't caught, but we think we know who they are, or we're all pretty clear what happened on 9/11, but there are still some mysteries.

Participatory Mode

Think Michael Moore as the most modern example of this type of documentary filmmaker. One of my favorite uses of this mode is *Dear Zachary*. You, the filmmaker, are part of the film. This mode is useful if you absolutely have an agenda. Michael Moore definitely has an agenda. He has a desired outcome for the viewer to come to. As part of the film, you have the opportunity to interject your own thoughts and opinions about what you are sharing. I find it hard not to be biased when using this mode, but it's possible for you to have an awakening or a change of heart, which is a great way to surprise your viewer.

Observational Mode

This is more like the viewer is a fly on the wall, observing events as they unfold and coming to their own conclusions about them. It claims reality and authenticity as its cornerstones. *War Photographer* (2001) is a great example of this. Director Christian Frei mounted a lipstick camera on the photographer James Nachtwey's camera to capture real-time footage of his movements and experiences. This is where documentary began and where it is most often today.

Nowadays, reality TV uses GoPros and diary cams. Essentially the camera is not impacting the events unfolding; it's capturing them. This is useful if you're going to be filming live events as they occur and then recapping or examining them from different perspective, but the audience also has their own perspective as they viewed the actual event in real time.

Reflexive Mode

To me, this is the toughest to explain. It's essentially reflecting on the process of filmmaking as an opportunity to reflect on one's thoughts on it . . . Huh? It's not used often, probably because no one understands it—here's the best example I've got (full disclosure—I pulled this from Wikipedia): "In Dziga Vertov's *Man with a Movie Camera* (1929), for example, he features footage of his brother and wife in the process of shooting footage and editing, respectively. The goal in including these images was 'to aid the audience in their understanding of the process of construction in film so that they could develop a sophisticated and critical attitude.'"[5]

Honestly, I have no idea what that means; it's very meta. *Meta* is the word of the day, these days . . .

> met·a
> /ˈmedə/
> *adjective*
> (of a creative work) referring to itself or to the conventions of its genre; self-referential.[6]

Other films that are considered meta or reflexive: *The Greatest Movie Ever Sold* (Morgan Spurlock), *My Date with Drew* (Brian Herzlinger), and *This Film Is Not Yet Rated* (Kirby Dick).

---

5   "Documentary Mode," *Wikipedia*, last modified April 1, 2019, https://en.wikipedia.org/wiki/Documentary_mode.

6   *English Oxford Living Dictionaries*, s. v. "meta," accessed April 29, 2019, https://en.oxforddictionaries.com/definition/meta.

Performative Mode

This can often be confused with the participatory mode, and some think *Dear Zachary* falls into this category, since the filmmaker is part of the process and the story is personal to him. He doesn't change the outcome; however, he has a relationship with his subject.

In this mode, the filmmaker's participation is deeply personal. Although not technically a documentary, Showtime's *High Resolution* follows a couple who make a documentary about their drug-infused romance. This is great if your story is about you, your life, or an event that you can share a personal experience around.

A film I was involved with, *Pregnant in America*, is a perfect example of this. It was made from the perspective of a first-time father, trying to find out if home birth is safe for his wife, a first-time mother. For me, as a second-time mother, having had both a hospital and home-birth experience, I had an agenda, somewhat of a biased agenda. It was personal. I think it's difficult to use this mode without being biased.

What does it mean to be biased?

> bi·as
> /ˈbīəs/
> *noun*
> Prejudice in favor of or against one thing, person, or group compared with another, usually in a way considered to be unfair.[7]

I personally find that definition to be a little rough. Being biased can be subtle. It's important to get clarity on your biases when making any type of film. This is an important conversation for you to have before you embark on your filmmaking journey. You don't have to give up your bias entirely, but you should be aware of it. Bias can come out while you are doing interviews, in what you choose to show or not show, and so on. When you're at least aware of it, you have the

---

7   *English Oxford Living Dictionaries*, s. v. "bias," accessed April 29, 2019, https://en.oxford-dictionaries.com/definition/bias.

opportunity to check in, to make sure your bias isn't impacting the film in a way that doesn't serve it.

So as you can see, there are multiple styles and they are not mutually exclusive to each other. Most films incorporate at least two of these styles. I find it's best to choose a motif, a gimmick, or one style and focus on it and incorporate other styles in a minimalistic way. Again, the film will lead you toward which style best suits its message. If you've done the work to get clarity around your who, what, when, where, and whys, your desired outcome, and your bias, then this decision should be easy. Check in with your mission and ask yourself, *Does this fit my mission?* The answer will be clear.

First-time filmmakers can become enamored with gimmicks, effects, overly cutty montages, motion graphics, or animations and end up overwhelming the viewer. This is a sign that you haven't done your research. You haven't fully listened to your film.

Take some time to decide if you intend to use graphics and in what style. Animations? Motion graphics? Just don't overdo it. This often doesn't become fully realized until you're in the editing room. And be prepared: That idea you had months ago before you started filming may not be what works in the end. Be willing to "kill your babies," as they say. Be willing to let the film evolve to what's ultimately "right."

Most important, and I'll quote Michael Moore here: "Don't make a documentary"; make a movie. Tell a story, because even if it's based on events that most everybody has the facts on, your goal is to inspire an emotional response, to connect emotionally with your viewer, and to engage them in your story. You can't do that when you're focused on techniques and gimmicks.

This may sound a bit woo-woo, but here it goes. I talk to my films. I get to know my film's personality. Is it funny, quirky, moody, emotional, erratic? Your story will usually tell you what's needed, what style will best convey your vision. Listen to it and get out of the way.

In addition to doing your research on the business side of making your documentary, learn storytelling. I suggest reading *Save the Cat*. I'm sure there are newer books about storytelling, but this and Joseph Campbell's *The Hero's Journey* are the two most important tools you need to tell a great story.

Save the Cat will teach you the basics of a three-act structure, and *The Hero's Journey* will give you a road map to follow for story beats and a pathway from beginning to end.

Joseph Campbell, in my opinion, is the greatest storyteller of all time. He understood the journey beyond the three-act structure. He outlines each step in a character's path toward the culmination of their journey. If you watch just about any good film, narrative, or documentary and you have an emotional response, you can watch it again and pinpoint every step of the hero's journey. Make a copy of the map shown here and then watch any *Star Wars* movie. Creator George Lucas has credited Joseph Campbell as a great influence on those films.

Initiation **Threshold** Apotheosis
Adventure **Crossing** Enter the Cave
Night Sea Journey Courage
Road of Trials Helpers
Magical Helper **FOLLOW** Belly of the Whale
Threshold Crossing **YOUR** **Threshold Crossing**
Fear **BLISS** Rescue
Separation Tests
Reluctant Hero Magical Flight
The Call Dragon Battle
Wasteland **Return**
Treasure

Another great documentary you can watch is *Finding Joe* (Patrick Takaya Solomon, 2011), a wonderful film about the hero's journey and what it means to follow your bliss.

Another fun assignment I gave my students was to examine a period of their life and track their own hero's journey. There is no better way to understand the powerful storytelling tool this is than to put it up against your own life, to experience it firsthand. This will help you find those moments in your film.

Trust me, you will hit the dark night of the soul.

Think of it this way: embarking on this journey to make your film is your call to action as a hero. You'll find the means somehow to make the film, and by reading this book, you're finding your mentors/helpers. During the filmmaking process, you'll face challenges and setbacks; you'll hit walls and experience the dark night of the soul. But if you're willing to move beyond this point, then you will have a moment of epiphany, a new awareness (this is the moment when you throw out the last cut and start over . . .), and you will finally understand what I mean when I say "You'll know when it's right." Others will agree with you, you'll release your film, and then regardless of the outcome, you will return home with wisdom and experience, be welcomed back into the fold triumphant, and then you'll start the process all over again.

That is the hero's journey in filmmaking. Welcome to it. Enjoy it. Savor every moment of it. What a gift to be able to have this journey. I am eternally grateful to have experienced it more than once.

Now we're on to the business of filmmaking.

CHAPTER 5

Business Plan Outline

OK, enough of the woo-woo . . . now let's get down to some brass tacks about what you will need to get that movie made.

What do you need to include in your pitch deck and your full business plan?

THINGS TO INCLUDE IN YOUR PITCH DECK

☐ **Elevator Pitch**—three sentences that describe your project. Make it intriguing and exciting and include a hook. They'll want to know more after reading it.

Example:

In 1963, NASA built seventeen space capsules, but only fifteen of them were made public. Join the journey to discover what happened to the other two.

☐ **Short Synopsis**—a one- to two-paragraph outline. Will your documentary be feature-length, a docuseries, or a short? Will its style be Poetic, Reflexive, Participatory, etc.?

☐ **Production Team**—a run-down of the producer, director, DP, and editor. You can dedicate one page to each team member (especially if they have other film credits) or list them all on one slide.

☐ **Key Participants**—a summary of the leading expert(s) on your subject and the interviews you have secured. Here, you can explain whether or not you have life rights for your subject.

☐ **Comparables**—a list of three films that are similar to yours and their revenues and or distribution. (For each, you can

include its film poster, revenue, and where it played, e.g.,
Netflix, Amazon, Hulu.)

☐ **The Market**—a short outline of your audience and why
they will flock to see your film. Stats and demographics in
short bursts. Limit yourself to three to five points—leave
the detail for the business plan.

☐ **Distribution Strategies**—a summary of whom you intend
to reach out to—theatrical, digital, both? Do you have strategic partnerships in place? Include anything that will make
your project seem more put-together, aligned with brands,
and show you have avenues for distribution. Of course—if
you have a deal, you should list it.

☐ **Sizzle Reel**—a link to your Sizzle Reel (a short intro trailer/
video to your project) if you have one. I highly recommend
investing in this. You will need it if you're planning on
applying for grants, and investors and crowdfunding will be
more successful if you have something to show them in the
form of a film. It doesn't have to be fancy, but it should be
slick and professional. If nothing else, create a digital look
book of your film.

Once people have viewed your pitch deck and have expressed serious interest in your project, you should first request they sign a nondisclosure agreement prior to sending them your full business plan.
This will help determine who's really interested or who just wants
to get a peek at your plans. As you'll see, I prefer to keep contracts
simple.[8]

---

8 A note about entertainment lawyers: I always advise people to have a lawyer. The documents that I provide in this book are templates and should be reviewed by your attorney.
Many reputable entertainment attorneys will review your documents or provide you with
templates at a reasonable cost. I typically budget between $3,000 and $10,000 in my budget for legal fees for more straightforward projects. This will cover things like crew deal
memos, nondisclosure agreements, the formation of your LLC, and basic agreements. If
you have a straightforward investor package, that amount should suffice. The more complicated you make things, the more expensive legal costs become. Always consult with an
attorney prior to using my or anyone else's templates.

Here is an example of a nondisclosure agreement:

MOVIE (FILM) NONDISCLOSURE AGREEMENT

WHEREAS, on the ____ of _____, 20____ this Movie Nondisclosure Agreement, hereinafter known as the "Agreement," is between _____, hereinafter known as the "Releasor," and _____, hereinafter known as the "Recipient," agree to the following:

I. The Project. All information disclosed about the movie, film, or script titled _____, hereinafter known as the "Project," that includes, but is not limited to, written, electronic, or oral statements made about the Project shall hereafter and forever be deemed confidential and shall further be known as "Confidential Information."

II. Ownership Rights. All Confidential Information shall remain the under the ownership of the Releasor with the Recipient agreeing not to disclose any information or ideas related to the Project except the Recipient's agents, licensees, successors, and assigns on a "need to know" basis. The Recipient shall be responsible for any improper disclosure of the Confidential Information by their representatives.

III. No Guarantees. This Agreement in no way guarantees or suggests employment for the Recipient or compensation for time as it relates to the development and evaluation of the Project. Should the Releasor resolve to employ the Recipient, no other contractual instruments may be applied.

IV. Severability. If any provision under this Agreement shall be held invalid or unenforceable for any reason, the remaining provisions and statements shall continue to be valid and enforceable.

IN WITNESS WHEREOF, the Recipient has executed this Agreement on the undersigned date.

Recipient's Signature: Date:

_____   _____

Print Name: _____

FULL BUSINESS PLAN

Once they have signed your nondisclosure agreement, you can share your full business plan, which includes all of the information in your pitch deck as well as budget and production schedule.

Budget (Including Marketing, Film Festivals, Delivery)

Review the sample budget on page 44 to get an idea of the items you should consider.

Production Schedule

When and where you intend to film, edit, and complete the film. Provide an estimated timeline including production, postproduction, film festivals, and target for release. This can either be in the form of a calendar or a PDF with important dates and milestones you intend to reach, including your goals for delivery and any film festivals or events you intend to make.

ROI/Expected Revenues

A little bit about ROI revenues and how to calculate them. The reality is, or at least the way I look at them, ROIs are essentially made-up numbers, best guesses, and high hopes. One can rarely predict the success of any project accurately, especially a film project in a very volatile market. I always advise filmmakers to be conservative, even with your high projections. (Check out a sample ROI sheet on page 45.) Clearly indicate on all ROIs and in your proposal that these are *estimated* projections and not a guarantee of profits or return on investment. You want to avoid making promises you may not be able to keep and that could come back to bite you in the butt with a lawsuit later. Your lawyer will also have language regarding investments and risks, which is essential to have in any information regarding ROI.

On page 46, you'll find an example of a Statement of Risk Factors. This is really for you to get a sense of what should be included. I strongly suggest that you consult with an attorney and request they draft language that reflects your specific project and the current laws regarding investments and securities. This should only be considered a starting point or reference.

BUDGET:

Description	Rate in $US	Quantity	Duration	Total Cost	In Kind	Cash
Budget Assumptions						
Shooting Formats:	Total Run Time(s):		Countries of Production:			
	Intended Delivery Date:		Currency of Production:			
Pre-Production | Research						
Proposal Development | Fund-raising	allow					
Archival Research						
Story Rights						
Story Consultant | Writer (Jamie Weil)	allow					
Research Shoot						
Sample Tape						
SUBTOTAL PRE-PRODUCTION | RESEARCH:				$		
Production						
Producer (Betsy Chasse/Jamie Weil)	allow					
Producer | Director (Betsy Chasse)	allow					
Director of Photography |						
Translator | Associate Producer | Fixer						
Consultants | Experts | Honoraria	allow					
Sound Recording						
Camera Package	allow					
Lighting & Equipment	allow					
Stock	allow					
Additional crew						
Airfare						
Hotel						
Meals						
Car Rental						
Gas | Parking | Mileage | Toll | Taxis - TRAVEL	allow					
SUBTOTAL PRODUCTION:				$		
Post-production						
Editor: Picture | Sound						
Assistant Editor						
Offline Editing Suite Rental						
Transcription Interviews	allow					
Archival Footage	allow					
Transfers and Conversions						
Edit Stock						
Masters						
Computer graphics | Titles	allow					
Animation	allow					
Online editing suite | Editor						
Original Music Composition | Recording	allow					
Sound Mix	allow					
SUBTOTAL POST-PRODUCTION:				$		
Outreach And Impact						
DVD Authoring						
DVD Dubs | Stock						
DVDCAM/Beta SP Screening Copies						
Poster | Press Kit | Materials	allow					
Shipping	allow					
Festival Entry Fees	allow					
Travel: Filmmakers and Subjects	allow					
Website: Design and Maintenance	allow					
Marketing (PR/Social)	allow					
Book and Other Ancillary Products	allow					
SUBTOTAL OUTREACH:				$		
Administrative Costs						
Bookkeeping	allow					
Legal Support	allow					
Overhead and Administrative Costs						
Contingencies	allow					
SUBTOTAL ADMINISTRATION:						
PROJECT TOTAL COSTS:				$		

(Title) Income Projections

($ Millions)	Notes	Low		Medium		High	
Domestic Theatrical Sales							
Box Office Gross		$	-	$	-	$	-
% Less Exhibitor/Theater share		$	-	$	-	$	-
Gross Film Rental		$	-	$	-	$	-
% Less Distributor Fee		$	-	$	-	$	-
Less Prints and Advertising		$	-	$	-	$	-
Domestic Theatrical Net Profit		$	-	$	-	$	-
Domestic Ancillary Sales							
Home Video/DVD		$	-	$	-	$	-
Pay Cable/TV		$	-	$	-	$	-
Network		$	-	$	-	$	-
VOD Streaming		$	-	$	-	$	-
Other		$	-	$	-	$	-
Gross Ancillary Sales		$	-	$	-	$	-
Less Distributor Fees		$	-	$	-	$	-
Domestic Ancillary Net Profit		$	-	$	-	$	-
Foreign Theatrical Sales							
Box Office Gross		$	-	$	-	$	-
Less Exhibitor/Theater Share		$	-	$	-	$	-
Gross Film Rental		$	-	$	-	$	-
Less Distributor Fee		$	-	$	-	$	-
Less Prints and Advertising		$	-	$	-	$	-
Foreign Theatrical Net Profit		$	-	$	-	$	-
Foreign Ancillary Sales							
Home Video/DVD		$	-	$	-	$	-
Pay Cable/TV		$	-	$	-	$	-
Network		$	-	$	-	$	-
VOD Streaming		$	-	$	-	$	-
Other		$	-	$	-	$	-
Gross Ancillary Sales		$	-	$	-	$	-
Less Distributor Fees		$	-	$	-	$	-
Foreign Ancillary Net Profit		$	-	$	-	$	-
Revenue and Profit							
Total Worldwide Revenue		$	-	$	-	$	-
Total Revenue After Taxes		$	-	$	-	$	-
Less Film Negative Costs		$	-	$	-	$	-
Total Net Profit		$	-	$	-	$	-
Total ROI		$	-	$	-	$	-

Sample Statement of Risk Factors

Investment in the film industry is considered high-risk and is highly speculative. Financial success cannot be assured for any motion picture, documentary, tele-film or series, or any other media product because the revenues derived from the production and distribution of said media product depend upon its acceptance by the public, which is unpredictable. There are other mitigating factors which can determine the success of a media product, such as the quality and acceptance of other competing media products released into the marketplace at or near the same time and general economic factors occurring in the world or where the product is released, among other tangible and intangible factors, all of which can change and cannot be predicted with certainty. In general, the entertainment industry—and particularly the motion picture industry—is in constant flux and change due to technological developments. These developments have resulted in the availability of alternative and competing forms of entertainment and distribution opportunities, as well as the creation of additional revenue sources via the licensing of rights to such new media. Furthermore, these developments could potentially lead to future reductions in the production and distribution costs of motion pictures and have created a market place flush with product, thus reducing the overall value of said product. A motion picture's theatrical success is still a vital factor in generating revenues in other media, such as home video products, television airings, digital downloads, and streaming services. It is impossible to predict the overall effect that the aforementioned factors, changeable consumer tastes, and the fluctuating popularity and availability of other forms of entertainment will have on the potential revenue from and profitability of feature-length motion pictures. Furthermore, the company in which you may invest is in the organizational/developmental stage and is subject to all the risks inherent in the creation and development of a new business, such as the lack of a history of operations, as well as minimal net worth and cashflow. In order to succeed, {your media product name} will depend partly upon the ability of the management team to produce a media product of exceptional quality at a lower cost or specified budget, which can compete in appeal with media products of the same genre. To minimize this risk, the management team will aim to mitigate financial risks where possible; this goal depends on the timing of investor financing and obtaining distribution contracts with satisfactory terms, as well as the current management's and/or producer team's ongoing participation.

The best way to calculate ROIs is to use your comparables. You can use sites like boxofficemojo.com or the-numbers.com to research revenues using their movie indexes. That will give you most films' revenues. Search your comparable film titles, and you should be able to find some data. If not, then you're going to have to become a detective, so pick up the phone or google all that you can. Budgets are rarely published; however, googling the film and reading articles, especially in the film trades, will generally mention some sort of budget amount. You can also contact the filmmaker. Some of them will be kind enough to share that information. I usually do. I'm not sure why filmmakers want to keep this information secret, unless it's to hide a failure or to exaggerate a success. With a little research, you can usually figure it out. Remember to check not only domestic revenues, but also foreign, digital, DVD, etc. As the number of platforms available increases, there are more avenues of revenues to discover. Digital (i.e., Amazon and Vimeo and other similar platforms) are the most difficult to deduce. You may have to make best guesstimates; be conservative! Again, you don't want to "overentice" your potential investor and leave yourself open for a lawsuit later. Better to underestimate and surprise everyone later than to overestimate and leave others wondering what happened to all those promises you made.

What if there are no other films like yours to compare to? This is probably not likely. Usually there are at least five to ten films that match your genre and documentary style and that can come close to the subject. If you're having a hard time, look at documentary revenues for the last five years in the markets and distribution platforms you're considering.

Google the search term "documentary revenues 2018" (or whatever year). I also like to check out statista.com, which can provide a bevy of excellent stats about the state of the film industry in general. The IDA is also producing a series, to come out every two years, called "The State of the Documentary Field," which will examine documentary trends, concerns and perspectives of documentary-industry professionals, new opportunities, projects in production, marketing, and distribution. I really suggest reading this to get the points of view of other professionals and a detailed understanding of the industry. They released a report in 2018 that is very informative. It's available online for free.

You could include the following quotes:

"There has never been a more profitable time for documentaries."

—IndieWire

"The global film industry shows healthy projections for the coming years, as the global box office revenue is forecast to increase from about 38 billion U.S. dollars in 2016 to nearly 50 billion U.S. dollars in 2020."

—Statista.com

Pulling quotes from articles that show potential for success is important, and you can show instances where there is growth, new platforms and distribution opportunities, etc. You want to paint a rosy picture for sure, and don't oversell it.

Here's an example of how to use a comparable:

Won't You Be My Neighbor? (2018)—made $22.6 million. Morgan Neville's portrait of Fred Rogers and *Mister Rogers' Neighborhood* proved to be a crowd-pleasing hit in the summer of 2018 because of the absolute niceness at its heart.

Our film on *Captain Kangaroo* shares the same type of heartwarming childhood icon and audience hungry for the nostalgia of their childhood.

Market and Marketing

This is a more detailed outline of your marketing strategy. Do you have specific contests, promotional events, or materials that will support your project? Do you have strategic partnerships with brands, organizations, nonprofits? Grants or crowdfunding? Outline those plans and arrangements. This can be a little bit of the cart before the horse. I tend to research and create alliances with partners before I go to investors. I have found that if the project is sound, and I have created a quality pitch deck, most strategic partners are willing to give letters of intent as long as the money comes through.

What is a letter of intent? This can come from any potential strategic partner or distributor you have connected with who agrees they will deliver on potential marketing partnerships and support if your film gets financed and completed to the level you've promised.

Examples of this: Does your film support a specific nonprofit or organization? Can you get a letter of intent that the organization will e-mail their client list about the film and/or do events and screenings of the film? Can you get a celebrity to be your narrator if you can pay them a certain salary? Will they support the film if it gets into certain film festivals or secures certain levels of distribution or financing?

Strategic alliances and celebrity endorsements are powerful tools to support your film. It may seem daunting, but doing a little research on what celebrity might be aligned with your project and finding ways to connect with them can change the trajectory of your project.

If I had a million dollars for every time I was asked "How do I get a celebrity attached to my project?" then I'd probably be a billionaire. Again, networking, networking, networking. What nonprofits do those celebrities support? Can you connect with those nonprofits? Will they help you connect with that celebrity? This is a careful dance, so don't appear too needy. This is all about establishing a trustworthy relationship and that takes patience. If you are authentic and truly aligned, then getting a celebrity will probably not be hard. It may not happen as you build your business plan, but make every effort to create whatever strategic alliances you can early on.

A caution about strategic alliances: Everyone has an agenda, especially nonprofits. Be sure not to make promises about content that you're not willing to live up to. This is extremely important because your film may not always align perfectly with their mission.

An example: I once distributed a film through my company that focused on alternative fuel. When we went out to release the film in theaters, we connected with many groups who all had a mission around the topic. What we found is that many would not support our film because it didn't completely align with their ideas about how to fix this problem. We had the audacity to share multiple ideas, and this wasn't OK with them.

I'll keep saying this: clarity, communication, expectations, and alignment of purpose. These are especially important when you're seeking partnerships of any kind.

I make sure everyone involved in my films is fully aware of whom I am interviewing, what areas I am exploring, and whether or not I am going to portray a philosophy or ideal different from theirs.

Here's a great story. In one of my films, I had scientists with tenure as well as mystics and channels . . . these people don't always line up. Before I interviewed anyone, I shared the bios of everyone in the film. I had them sign a very concrete agreement that indicated I would not change the context of their words or change their meaning, and they had the opportunity to remove themselves from the film at any time. I shared cuts with everyone I interviewed. The film was released, pushback came from the hard-core scientific community, and one scientist tried to say I twisted their words. I did not. They got theoretical when their "accepted work" was not. I had the full transcripts, and I did not alter their intention, meaning, or words. When their community pushed back on them, they claimed otherwise and said they would sue me.

I stated back: I am happy to release the contract, all of our communication, and the transcripts of their interview for full disclosure. They shut up . . . immediately. My point here is, cover your ass. Operate with integrity and authenticity, and you will probably have no issues.

Give details about your audience research and statistics on the market. For example, if your film is about health and wellness products, you could include the statistic that in 2015, $20 billion was spent on health and wellness products in the US, and $5 billion of that was spent on entertainment and education. (Always site references.) You can usually find this type of information by simply googling "market share" or "market statistics" in whatever your topic is. Explain how this information relates to your project and how it supports your budget and ROI.

This is where your who, what, when, where, and whys come into play. The more you can show that you know your audience and how to reach them (i.e., you have a detailed plan of how to do this and a realistic budget), the more likely you are to get investors.

Distribution Plan

You can suggest that you have multiple plans depending on what outcome best suits the project at completion. I generally don't put too much emphasis on theatrical unless I already have a deal. You could suggest a limited theatrical release based on your market research that shows that theatrical screenings in certain markets would boost video on demand (VOD) numbers.

If you have deals in place—great! If you don't, avoid listing every possible platform. Choose the ones you think best suit your project and why. Be honest here. Look, distribution is a gambler's bet, especially right now. We are in the Wild Wild West of distribution, and sometimes a theatrical deal is the death of your project. Here, I tend to say, "Hey, I have no idea who's going to buy this project, but I know it will be bought. Here's why. . . . "

Why would Hulu be better than Netflix? (FYI: None of my films are on Netflix. Unless I can make a deal with Netflix premiere, Netflix is where films go to die a slow, nonmonetary death unless they are actually bought or produced by Netflix.) This is tough because you want to be able to show your film is going to be seen and potentially make money, but there are no guarantees. This is the place to be honest and conservative. What is the best-case scenario and the worst case? Show how you've budgeted for the middle ground.

List the film festivals you intend to enter and the schedule for them. Most film festivals prefer that you have not released the film beforehand, so a film festival run will hold up any chance at generating revenues but it might help with securing a distribution deal. Especially for documentaries, film festivals are your best chance for getting a deal.

This is the perfect place to show, regardless of your distribution, that you, independently, have built an audience for your film. I start my social platforms as early as possible to generate a following for the film as the film is in production, appearing at film festivals, etc. Eventually your film will make its way to some platform, and you'll want people to be excited to see it.

Although you are still building your plan, adding in information about your social media strategies are helpful.

What are your plans for social media? How will your strategic partnerships and social media platform help build awareness for your film? What platforms are best suited for your audience? The goal is to show potential partners and investors that you have thought through the many aspects of bringing your film to life.

Marketing and distribution are a world of their own. As I said earlier, *Bleep* launched the same day Facebook did in 2004. In order to generate that audience, I didn't have social media as it is today. I spent time getting to know my audience. Where they were at. I built a marketing plan to reach them based on tons of research. I broke all the rules in terms of where to open and when. It worked because I understood who would see my film, why they would see it, and how much they would spend to see it. If you can share a compelling reason, then you don't have to promise HBO: you just have to promise an audience.

That is why doing your research, understanding the who, what, when, where, and whys and putting it together in a cohesive business plan will not only open your eyes to what's possible or not, but it will also support you in getting the funding and team you need to execute your vision successfully.

MONEY, MONEY, MONEY!

SECTION III

NOW YOU HAVE A PLAN. You just need to fund it! As they say, there are a million ways to skin a cat, and there are a million ways to fund your project, the easiest being that you're independently wealthy and have an endless supply of cash to throw at your project. This is rare. It's more likely you're going to need to get an investor, crowdfund, borrow money from a family member, or apply for grants, or all of the above or even a combination of the above. Figuring out what best suits you, your financial goals, and the project are important.

In the coming chapters, I will explore how to approach each of these options. Right now, let's explore how to determine which is best for your project. Each has its own pros and cons.

Let's start with borrowing money from a family member. This is the most common way to fund your project, especially if you're a first-time filmmaker, the budget is low, and your family wants to support you in your career. It's also often the easiest. Your family knows you, they probably trust you, and they have a desire to see you succeed. These are all the pro reasons for family support.

On the con side—borrowing money from family and not having clear agreements and expectations can cause a lot of upset and grief, not just for you and the family member you borrowed money from. It can have a rippling effect throughout your family. First and foremost, it's important to be clear about this possibility and make sure you have a plan to avoid it. Some things to avoid: don't borrow money from your dad or uncle without their wives or partners aware of the loan. Make sure this family member can live without the money they are lending if you are not able to pay them back.

Treat this as you would any other type of business deal. Have a contract that clearly spells out all your expectations and theirs. In addition to outlining how much money they are giving you and how it will be paid back, clarify their involvement in the film creatively and in any profit sharing. Is this a straight-up loan with interest to be paid back in a certain time frame? Or are they acting more as an investor, understanding risks associated with investing? Do they have any creative say in the project? Are they requiring you to hire their kid? You may think I'm being silly and yet asking all these questions, having a very detailed conversation, and putting it all in writing will save you from dealing with upset later.

After running your ROI and examining your profitability, do you feel strongly that your film has enough potential to generate funding from an investor or investors? What type of structure are you willing to create? Typically, investors require that they recoup their initial investment plus receive what's called a bump (usually 15 to 20 percent on top of their investment), then a profit share of 50 percent of the investors' pool. Think of it like this. Your film is split into two halves of a pie: 50 percent goes to the investors and the other 50 percent to the producers (that's your share). You may end up giving away pieces of your share to others (cinematographers, composers, other producers) as an incentive for them to work for less, and the investors' pool is split between all the investors based on their contribution. If your budget is $100,000 and one investor puts in $75,000 and another only puts in $25,000, then the bigger investor gets a bigger piece of his side of the pie, 75 percent of the pie to be exact.

How many investors are you willing to work with? What type, if any, of creative control are you willing to give them? Do they have a say in finalizing distribution deals or sales of the film? Ask yourself, *What is this money worth to me? Is it worth it at all?* Sometimes investments can actually cost too much. For instance, if you can get $100,000—your entire budget—from one investor, but he wants a 25 percent bump and the entire 50 percent of the investors' share, plus creative control and his niece to be your directing partner, is it worth it? It may be better to find two investors or you may be able to get a piece of the investor pool carved out for yourself. These deals can get complicated, and as I have said, this is where you really must work with a reputable attorney. This is not the place for you to skimp or do it yourself. Playing with other people's money never is.

Should you crowdfund? Crowdfunding sounds sexy and fun. I'm here to tell you it's not. Crowdfunding used to be an easy way to get quick "free" cash to make your film; unfortunately, it's been around for years, so people are not as likely to shell out $10 for an autographed poster like they used to. This is a full-time job and a huge endeavor to undertake. I'll go over how to crowdfund in a later chapter, but unless you have a huge following, an enormous mailing list, and lots of friends, aunts, uncles, and cousins, it's not likely you'll raise more than $5,000 to $10,000 here. I will say, if you're looking to fund a small amount like that, or you're looking for seed money to get started, create a sizzle reel, or hire a lawyer, then crowdfunding can be a useful tool.

Grants are a great way to fund your project, if you have patience and time. They take a while to generate, and most grants have very specific requirements to be fulfilled in order to get the funds. Most grants are usually given to filmmakers with a proven track record or who are aligned with a specific cause or group (i.e., gender, LGBTQ rights, minority issues, etc.). Rarely will you find a grant that covers your entire production and marketing/distribution budget.

Strategic partnerships are also a way to find funding. Can you work with a nonprofit or an organization that is in alignment with your subject, allowing them to use the film to support their cause (i.e., to share in profits or to use as a fund-raising tool)? This is also helpful if you choose to go the crowdfunding route. You can align with groups that have big e-mail lists; sharing the funds can help get you the reach you need to make your goal.

It's likely you're going to use more than one of these ways to fund your film. There are other ways, like tax credits or small business loans, which can also be utilized. For independent documentaries, these avenues are unlikely and not often worth the trouble. You should be as creative with how you fund your project as you are in the content. There is no "one way" or "right way." It's the way that works best for your project.

Don't be too quick to take money simply because it shows up. Take the time you need to run all the numbers, create a clear contract, have it reviewed by a lawyer, and, most important, check in with your gut. If you don't feel 100 percent confident in the deal you're about to sign, do not sign it. There is nothing worse than taking someone's money, spending it, and regretting it later.

There are several types of funding opportunities if you're seeking an investor.

- **Equity:** This is hard cash given to you by an investor or a group of investors. They will require an equity stake in the film (the investors' share) and they will want to be paid back before any profits are shared.
- **Presales:** This isn't usually an option for an independent doc—however, it is possible. Perhaps your documentary is based on a historical figure from a specific country. Can you presell the film to a distributor in that country or to a cable or TV network that will air it? Can you pre-sell it to a Netflix or to HBO? In this scenario, usually the buyers either become the production company and fund the project or they give you a letter of intent, which you then take to a bank or another lender, who buys the note.
- **Gap:** Gap is when you've raised some money and are looking for finishing funds or completion funds. There are companies who will finish a film for a stake in ownership. This can get tricky because often they will want to be the first paid back, and you'll need to get approval from your investors to put someone else ahead of them in the payback line. You could also get a gap loan from a bank. Of course, this is like any other type of loan. They will want collateral (usually the film), and the film will need to pretty much be a shoo-in for recouping.
- **Mom/Dad/Uncle Joe:** This pretty much speaks for itself.
- **Deferred:** This is basically agreeing to pay everyone from the profits of the film. You may be able to accomplish this with your sizzle reel, but it's a hard road to embark on for your entire film. Ultimately, it depends on your relationships with the people you'll need to make your film.

I try to stick with private equity as much as possible. I like one angel investor (a person who is especially passionate about my film) I can manage. I start a project with my own funds and then raise finishing funds. The fewer people I have to pay back, deal with, get approvals from, or report financials to, the better.

Do not mortgage your house to make a movie!

I have seen this before, and it never ends well. . . . OK, I probably shouldn't say *never*. There are probably a couple of case studies that show it working out . . . but it's very rare. Do not go into debt unless you have means to pay it back regardless of the success of your film.

Running out your line of credit, risking your property and/or the property of your family is not a way to fund your film. If you cannot afford to lose it, don't spend it.

CHAPTER 6

To Sizzle or Not to Sizzle?

What is a sizzle reel? It's a bit like a trailer for a film you haven't shot yet. It's also more specifically designed to be seen by potential investors or other partners, used in your crowdfunding campaign or with your grant proposals.

Again, knowing your audience is key when creating your sizzle reel. You want to be able to convey the look and feel of your documentary as well as the genre and subject matter, and you want it to be as high-end as you can afford. It's made to impress those watching it enough that they'll open their wallets or sign on to the project in some other way. Typically, a sizzle reel is longer than a trailer. It can be five minutes or even up to fifteen minutes. For some grants, you're required to have at least thirty minutes of your film edited to apply.

You can either shoot a couple of interviews and edit a section of your film or produce a concept reel using stock footage. The most important thing to remember: whatever you create, make it look great. If you can't film something yourself and make it look top-notch, it's better to not have a sizzle reel at all. Less can be more here. You can always wow them with a look book.

If you're going for an investor, the more you can shoot yourself and edit, giving them a true feeling of how the film will look, the more likely you'll get an investor.

The reality today is that investors have high expectations, and you have a lot of competition, so if you can't get it together to film a sizzle reel, then you probably can't get it together to make a film. Making a sizzle reel is a good test of your ability and commitment to making an entire film. It doesn't have to cost an arm and a leg. Typically, I spend about $3,000 to $5,000 on my sizzle reels. I either fund this myself or I crowdfund that portion of my process. This is eventually recouped out of my budget when I am funded. I also create a one-page website where the short synopsis, my contact information, and the sizzle reel are available for people to easily view.

Here is an example of a sizzle reel I created for one of my narrative projects: http://bit.ly/KBreel.

I filmed an actress for one day in a black-box theater and then intercut her with "borrowed" footage from films and old movies. This allowed the viewer to experience the genre, the tone, the look, and the feel the movie would eventually have.

If you're hoping to crowdfund, in addition to some sort of sizzle or trailer, you're going to need to film your "ask" or your "pitch." This is where having your mission, your *why,* is key. Especially for crowdfunding, people want to know your story, why are you making this film, what is your desired impact. They want to meet the team and feel as if they are a part of the project.

This can be you on camera, other members of your team, or the subject of your film—anyone who can convey a sincere message and be accessible enough that people will want to donate to your project.

Have you noticed lately that at the beginning of films, especially Disney films, the filmmakers and/or actors are saying thank you for coming to see the film? This is because audiences desire to be more connected to a film; they want more than just to watch it once and be done. This is especially true if you're going to crowdfund.

CHAPTER 7

Securing Investors

Does your film have the potential to earn a lot of money? (Or even break even?) This is a really big question, and it's time to be realistic. You've run a basic ROI, you've done a budget, and now it's time to figure out where the money is going to come from. Even if you're self-funded, understanding the money is key to your success. Are you going to look for investors, and if so, who, where, how, and what's the deal?

I'm back to my favorite Ws again. Who is your ideal investor? Is it someone who's passionate about the subject matter? This is usually referred to as an angel investor: someone who believes in the message or the cause or who has a personal relationship to the story.

Pros of an angel investor: it starts with the name—they are usually angels! They are excited, supportive, and most of the time not as focused on getting their money back or at least not in a hurry. They probably know other people who are as excited about the subject as they are. They can provide not only monetary support but also great connections for you in other ways (e.g., potential interview connections, strategic partners).

Cons of an angel investor: They are emotionally invested in the outcome, which can actually be worse than a straight financial risk. They often want some sort of creative control and have an agenda, so as always be clear about roles and expectations.

An angel investor can also mean someone from your family. As I discussed before, treat it like any other business relationship. Forget you've known them your entire life and do everything as if you've just met them and don't know them. The reality is, when dealing with money, we probably don't even know our own mother.

Is your ideal investor a business person, looking to put up capital in order to make a return on their investment or have a loss for a couple of years?

Pros of having a venture capitalist or professional investor: they know the drill, they won't waste your time, and they know what they want and are willing to walk away if they don't get it. They understand the risk they are taking and are less likely to be drawn in by fancy talk and bright colors. They will usually ask a lot of questions and have you deal with their financial liaison who will vet your project. Be prepared and professional.

Cons of working with a professional investor: They usually want their money back, and they will watch you like a hawk. Their money is usually more expensive than an angel investor's. They will want to see every aspect of your business plan and how you intend to market the film, and they will likely check up on you often. You'll be required to deliver financial reports, and you may need to hire an experienced accountant to provide what they are looking for.

They will likely run a credit check and a background check, so if you have any skeletons in your closet, it's best to be honest about them up front. For example, I got divorced and filed for bankruptcy. It wasn't a pleasant time in my life, and my credit was awful. I was still able to get investors because I was honest about my situation from the beginning; many people these days have gone through a divorce, and they know the mess it makes of your credit score; and I had great references and a solid track record.

In any of the scenarios above, it's all about the deal. How much is the money going to cost you and what will you be giving up in order to get it? This is a good time to be prepared to walk away from something if it doesn't feel right. Better to say no than to regret it later. It's tough because you need the money, but don't sell yourself short out of desperation. Be patient. If your project is put together well and you've done your homework, it will happen. This is your most important relationship.

I have reviewed the standard producer/investor pools, the fifty-fifty split, and how those pools are divided within themselves. The other areas of consideration are the bump—the money your investor wants above and beyond their investment as a return (no more than 20 percent)—plus ownership/copyright, approvals, and final cut, etc. There are many different aspects to an investor agreement, and as I keep advising, do not do this without good legal representation.

I will review some of these categories and hope that you will heed my advice and hire a good lawyer. I will not give you an example investor agreement because I've never really found a good "standard investor contract." If you're working with someone else's money, hire a lawyer.

The bump is essentially the money an investor wants to make back in addition to the money they gave you. If they give you $100,000 and they ask for a 20 percent bump, then you're expected to return $120,000. I have heard of higher bumps and premiums, but I won't pay them; the money becomes too expensive. I'd rather work with two to three investors than one who wants more than I can expect to earn (paying them back the initial investment, then a bump, and then giving them 50 percent of the profits).

Ownership/copyright: I recommend you create an LLC specifically for your project. This protects you and any other assets you might personally have from any potential lawsuit in which you could be held financially liable. The LLC also becomes the owner of the copyright. There may be language in your investor agreement about what happens if you don't pay them back and who gets to own the film, but it's never owned by you or them outright. It's owned by the LLC.

People try to get fancy with their LLC filings and go to Nevada or Delaware. I don't. Most of my work will most likely be done in California, and I'll still end up paying taxes there, so make it easy on yourself.

Other reasons to start a separate LLC is because beyond your investor agreement you may be hiring crew, etc., and may be required to purchase workman's compensation insurance or other liability insurance, and you want to limit your liability to only the LLC and the film.

Approvals: What type of approvals does the investor get? Do they have a say in the final cut? Do they have the right to reedit the film? Do they have the right to approve contracts (deals with key crew, distribution agreements)? These are all important pieces for you to consider when entering into an agreement with an investor. This may be someone you don't know very well, so how much power and control are you willing to give up for their money?

Typically, I give final cut to the investor if I have the right to remove my name from the film when I don't agree with their edits or suggested edits. Giving them final cut with a clear set of guidelines, approvals, remedies for issues, and a clear set of expectations means that usually I won't have to do this.

This goes back to my earlier discussion about having very honest conversations about expectations. Get to know the people who are investing in your film. If they have invested in others, talk to those filmmakers. Make friends with their staff and people around them. You will probably have many conversations with their assistant. Get chatty and they will probably leave you breadcrumbs for how the person operates. Research them to see how many lawsuits they've been involved with and why. Just because they have money to give you and may seem successful doesn't mean they are the right fit for you and your project. Be willing to say no and wait for the person or persons who are. This relationship is too important not to check in with your gut and Google.

It's also important if you're working with multiple investors to try to keep the agreements on an even playing field. Stick with percentages: in other words, the percentage of their investment against your budget equals the percentage of their profits, their bump, their control.

And the big question—where do I find an investor?

It's most likely going to be someone you know, either personally or through a networking contact. This is where your schmoozing skills come into play. There is no place that is specifically organized or called the Film Investor Warehouse.

But there are networking groups. There are also venture capital events where you can pay a fee, go pitch your project, and hope for the best. You will most likely find connections to funding through people who are interested in your subject matter, have a desire to be a part of bringing it to life, and have money. Unlike narrative-feature makers, who have an easier time finding funding because they have an easier formula and pathway to their ROI, documentary filmmakers have to spend more time looking in out-of-the-ordinary places for an investor. I call it turning over rocks.

Every film I have been a part of has been funded by someone who was passionate about the subject. I found them by talking to people, a lot of people. It helps that I had a track record as a line producer for feature films for twenty years and had made a couple of very successful documentaries. If it's your first time, then having a solid business plan and showing up prepared will help; teaming up with someone who has a track record helps too. Or ask your dentist. I'm not kidding. Dentists usually have a lot of excess cash and for some reason like being involved in films. People with other professions like to diversify. Sometimes in order to balance out their own tax liabilities, they need to place funds somewhere not yet earning a profit.

Don't be shy and don't be surprised if your uncle's dentist invests. I have seen investors come from the most unexpected places.

CHAPTER 8

Crowdfunding

About ten years ago, crowdfunding was where it was at. It was new and exciting, and you had the potential to raise hundreds of thousands of dollars for a project. Now, not so much.

Crowdfunding is a huge undertaking. It requires a budget and marketing plan of its own. Crowdfunding is successful based on two things: content and eyeballs. The going theory is that you need one hundred people to even look at your campaign in order to get one $25 contribution.

And it's not even $25 that you will get in the end. You need to budget for credit-card fees, processing fees, and whatever fee your crowdfunding platform is charging.

There are several platforms all with different ways to generate funds. The basic and most recognized are Kickstarter and Indiegogo. They have two avenues for crowdfunding: all or nothing, or what you get.

All-or-nothing funding basically means you must raise all the funds you've asked for or you don't get any of it. If crowdfunding is your only source of funding and you won't do the project unless you raise it all, this is your best choice.

What-you-get funding means that whatever you raise you get. If you make your goal, the percentage the crowdfunding platform takes is usually lower than if you don't. If you have other funding sources and you're using crowdfunding as a supplement to your budget, then use this option.

There are other sites such as Seed&Spark, which also allows for you to get donations, such as airline miles, and donated services, such as camera gear or PR/marketing services. Each of these is assigned a monetary value, which helps you get your goal, even if it's in in-kind donations and not actual cash.

I don't have a preference because I don't think it really matters. What matters most is your ability to get as many people as possible to check out your campaign and that your project resonates with them. What also matters is that have you budgeted realistically, done your research to make sure there is an audience for your film, and you know how to find them.

Here's a reality check: open your Facebook account and scroll through your feed. Just about everybody is raising money for something, so you'll have to get beyond that noise in order to get people to even click on your campaign.

People are donation weary. I've already donated this month to a cat rescue, a liver transplant, a friend who has cancer. Why on earth would making your film be more important than that?!

One option I like to use is to partner with a nonprofit. You could even get a fiscal sponsorship with a nonprofit. This way, the donations given are actually charitable and people can use it as a write-off. (Sadly, this option may be fading out since our new tax laws make this harder to achieve.) There are a couple of places that do this: From the Heart Productions and Creative Visions, which act just like a crowdfunding platform except they are a nonprofit and you don't have to come up with all the perks and giveaways needed for regular crowdfunding platforms.

Your fiscal sponsor holds the 501(c)(3) paperwork and has partnered with you. They are responsible for filing all the taxes and providing the tax-deductible receipts to the donators. You are responsible for whatever taxes relate to the funds you actually receive.

If you choose fiscal sponsorship, you don't have to work with only nonprofits who do films; you could do this with any nonprofit as long as you and they enter into a fiscal-sponsorship agreement. This might be great if your film has a specific cause or message relating to a nonprofit who has a large e-mail list or access to grant funding.

The most important part of crowdfunding is how many people can you reach and what level of financial commitment/gift can they give you.

Most $100,000 campaigns are funded by around forty to fifty people. That means that people are contributing (FYI: in straight crowdfunding without nonprofit status, the funders are making a contribution, not a donation) at levels ranging from $10 to even $2,500 or $5,000.

You will need to start by making a list of everyone you know and everyone your team knows and categorizing them in terms of how much you think they could contribute. Each of these levels will require a different ask. You will have those you connect with via social media, and they are your low-hanging fruit. Then you will have those you can ask for more money from. Those people require a more personal touch. Personal e-mails directly related to each person (*"Dear John, I saw your daughter made the high school varsity soccer team—that's great! I am really excited to share about a project I am working on that I am very passionate about . . ."*).

It's also important not to overdo the schmooze. Be as personal as you would typically be with them, and be straight up and authentic. Asking people for money can feel awkward and uncomfortable, especially if you haven't done it much. I find not beating around the bush and being realistic actually works. Don't ask for $2,500 when you know they can't give it. I'd rather ask ten people I know who can spare $100 than to ask one person for $1,000 who may not be able to give it. I've also found that when I ask authentically for $100, some people actually give more.

Don't get caught up in the myth that if you post it on social, they will come. They probably won't, and you're going to have to harass the bejesus out of people for up to thirty days in order to reach your goal. Crowdfunding is not a sprint: it's a marathon.

Be ready for daily posts (sometimes hourly) with update videos, press releases, and big shout-out thank-yous to your bigger contributors.

As I mentioned before, you'll need some sort of sizzle reel and a short video with you and other people attached to the project sharing their whys: why you are making it, why it is important, why they should give up hard-earned money for you . . .

Your perks don't need to be extravagant. The reality is, most people don't contribute for the perks; they contribute because they like you, know you, want to support you, or are passionate about the subject. Offer simple things you don't have to manufacture and ship; otherwise you're spending the money delivering those items that you could be putting into your film. For bigger donors, giving an associate producer credit, a part in the film, or an invitation to the premiere are great options. Just remember, whatever you promise, you need to deliver, and the less you have to pay for it, the better.

Unless you can get your sizzle reel and other videos and graphics for free, expect that your crowdfunding campaign will cost you about $2,500 to $10,000, depending on how much you want to raise. In addition to budgeting for the credit-card and processing fees, budget for your sizzle reel, your graphics—poster and other visuals—social media marketing, website design, hosting, perk creation and delivery, legal fees, and taxes. You may want to hire a publicist, or you can pay Newswire to send out your press release (this can cost between $600 and $1,500). If you can do it, I highly suggest hiring a publicist. Remember, it's all about how many people you can get to visit your campaign, and every little bit helps. If you can't hire a publicist, become your own. Contact your local news media, radio stations, and public-radio hosts, and write op-ed pieces about your subject (these can't overtly promote your campaign, but they can increase awareness about your subject). All these places need content, and if you can craft a compelling short story for them to fill their airtime and that is relevant to their audience, you're likely to get some press. There is literally a podcast for everything these days. I have had a lot of success in reaching out to indie podcasters aligned with my subject, appearing on their show and raising a few hundred dollars, at least, from that appearance. Every penny counts, especially when you're crowdfunding.

As I mentioned before, I would not suggest going for your entire budget in a crowdfunding campaign, unless your budget is under $30,000, and you have a big enough audience that you can easily reach out to upward of two thousand people.

Some people opt to do multiple campaigns, one for production, one for postproduction, and one for marketing and distribution. Ultimately this depends on your budget.

If you need $15,000, then ask for that *plus* whatever your crowd-funding costs are so that you can pay for both. Be prepared for a lot of action in the beginning, a slowdown toward the middle, and hopefully a mad rush to the finish line. People like to be a part of something successful. I usually line up all my bigger contributors prior to even launching the campaign and then I pepper them throughout. It gives people a reason to get excited, especially when things look as if they are slowing down. Prior to launching my campaign, I try to secure a couple of big contributors ($1,000–$5,000). I usually start off the campaign with the smaller of these contributors ($1,000–$2,000), then a bigger contributor ($2,000–$5,000), and then hopefully I can drop one in the middle and one on the last day or so to heat up the excitement. The idea is to spread some of your larger contributors throughout the campaign, some in the beginning, some in the middle, and some at the end. A typical campaign is thirty days. I don't suggest going longer, or your friends on social media will get tired of you. Only go shorter if you already have a good amount of people ready to contribute.

A word about consultants. As with anything, you get what you pay for. There are tons of companies and consultants who offer crowd-funding campaign-management services and/or social media market-ing services. A good one can be worth their weight in gold; sadly, most of them aren't. If you have the money to hire a consultant, you are probably better off hiring a good lawyer or publicist. I suggest spend-ing a few hundred dollars doing meetings with good ones or taking an online course and getting as much info as you can from them. There are also tons and tons of great how-to articles and videos that will cost you nothing but a little of your own time doing the research. After years of giving other people money and not always getting back what I expected, I took the time to learn about social media marketing, crowdfunding, and other aspects of the process I usually paid a con-sultant for. Now I consult for people who don't want to spend thou-sands they don't have, and I help them become empowered to do it themselves. I do, on occasion, pay for a course or hire someone for an hour of their time if I have specific questions and can maximize my time with them. An honest consultant, one who wants you to succeed, will offer a reasonably priced Q and A session where you come prepared with a list of questions they will answer. All of them (including me) will try to upsell you. If it feels right, you gained some wisdom from your initial meeting, and you feel you could benefit from continuing to work with them, go for it. If not, don't feel that because you may be inexperienced, you need them. And once again, create a very clear contract about what you are paying for and what they will do and not do. If they promise you or make any guarantees, get it in writing.

If you already have a good network, you might consider skipping the crowdfunding platforms altogether and create a way for people to contribute without having to pay all the fees. You'll still need to pay taxes and any credit-card processing fees. Once you set up your LLC, open a bank account; set it up with PayPal, Venmo, Stripe, or any other payment-processing platform; set up the parameters and legal declaimers (you can look at what other crowdfunding sites do), and do it yourself. As long as you are clear about what people are contributing to and follow the law and rules for crowdfunding, why give your money to someone else? You will probably want to create a website. Again, this isn't as difficult as one might think. I use WordPress sites and build them myself. Nowadays, you can easily drag and drop everything you need. You need a basic site that can support your YouTube video(s), a page about the film, a page about the team, and page for people to contribute. You can find a free WordPress template, or you can buy one for about $50 that has everything you need. If you're technologically challenged, do not spend more than $1,500 on your website if you hire outside help.

Another option is hosting a fund-raiser of your own, at a local restaurant, a bar, or your house. If you can connect with a hundred people who would each be willing to contribute $100, you've just raised $10,000. That may sound daunting; however, if you consider the money, energy, and time you are going to put into a traditional crowdfunding campaign, it's actually a whole lot easier and more fun.

I have had more success with creating personal experiences via private events than bombarding my social network and e-mail lists begging for money for my projects. And since it seems everyone is now in the fund-raising game, doing something unique or outside of the box will show people that you might just have the chutzpah to make it in showbiz. As I said, you need to find a way to stand out from the crowd. Getting out from behind your computer, shaking hands, and kissing babies is a great place to start when raising funds.

A crowdfunding campaign can be wonderful way to jump-start your project or to finish it. It's also great if you have a very small budget, a solid network of friends who want to support you, and the energy and time to manage it properly. It's also a useful tool in terms of building awareness for your project and beginning your marketing and social media platform. Even if people don't contribute financially, one of the benefits of a crowdfunding campaign is building your social media presence. People may like your page and begin to follow you in order to keep up with the project. Raising even a small amount of money will show future investors that you are serious and that there is interest in your project. It can build social currency for your film.

You can turn your social platform into dollars, either by using it to show interest in your project to investors or as leverage with potential strategic partners. As with everything, have a clear set of goals and expectations and then focus on achieving them. For example, some great, realistic goals would be raising $10,000 as starting or finishing funds; building your social platform, networking and connecting with others who can support your film; or paying for the crowdfunding campaign. Make your choices and decisions with those goals in mind and it's likely you'll have a successful campaign. Timing is everything, and if part of your funding strategy is to use crowdfunding, best to start late January to September. At the end of the year, it's harder to get people to pay attention.

CHAPTER 9

Grants and Alternative Funding Sources

Besides having an investor or doing a crowdfunding campaign, there other ways to fund your film. Many filmmakers take advantage of the thousands of grants offered for films. Grants are essentially money given to a project without the expectation of being repaid. Grants often have very specific guidelines and requirements. Some grants specifically want a certain amount of diversity, grants for women filmmakers, minority filmmakers, foreign, domestic, specific causes, or messages.

You can research grants online. Most major trades have yearly updated lists of what grants are available and when they are open for submissions. The IDA has a pdf of every grant available. It's updated often.

Grants seem like they are the panacea for funding films. Upon reading many of them, one would think they are the perfect match! The trick to receiving grants is in the grant writing, to strictly adhering to their guidelines for submission, and applying to as many as you can. Remember there are probably thousands of other filmmakers applying for the same grant. They take time to pay out, and they will have specific requirements around reporting, delivery, film festivals, distribution, other investors. . . . Be thorough in reviewing all their requirements before you take the time to apply.

Grant writing is an art form all its own. There are people who do this for a living, and there are courses you can take that will give you some tips and tools in preparing your grant. Again, it's all in how you "sell it," and the people who are approving grants have seen it all. Be honest about where you are at, put your best foot forward, and spell-check!

There are grants for development and preproduction; however, most grants will want to see something visual, like a trailer or a teaser; for some, you will need to show at least thirty to forty minutes of a rough cut of your film. Grants should be treated the same way you would approach an investor. Not only will they require a complete business plan, but they may also have other requirements, such as at least one key team member who has completed a film. They may ask if you are working with a qualified mentor or if you have a producer who is supporting you and overseeing the project, even if it's not on a day-to-day basis.

Grants go to those filmmakers who (1) can show they will complete their project, (2) have the team and the skills already in place, (3) fit the criteria perfectly, and (4) are a very low risk. And even with all of that, it's a crapshoot. If you're hoping to receive a grant as part of your funding package, you should apply for as many as you can.

You can apply for and receive multiple grants. It's possible to fund your entire project through grants, although it's not likely. Diversify, diversify, diversify!

Again, look at grants as a potential piece of your funding package. In addition to the bigger grants, look for smaller grants or grants for goods and services. Usually, they are easier to apply for and receive.

In addition to your typical grants, there are lots of contests for filmmakers that can provide you with prize money, camera gear, and other things you may need. Often major corporations will run contests for shorts and commercials that award the winner with not only exposure, but also with stuff you need. If you have the ability to shoot something short and easy that can get their attention, it might be easier and more fun than filling out grant applications. This will also help with potential investors. Winning awards and grants shows them you're serious and have talent.

Look outside of the film industry for other types of grant funding. Many organizations offer funding to filmmakers who will make a film or an ad for them. Walmart may have a grant for a filmmaker looking to promote their green initiatives—could you accommodate this into your project? If it is in alignment, can you create a strategic partnership with them or another organization or nonprofit? If you have all the gear and the crew, can you make a thirty-second or three-minute piece that helps you get additional funding for your project?

Be creative.

Strategic partnerships can generate funding and also an easier pathway to distribution. Aligning with organizations that already have a platform and audience for your project can help with applying for grants, seeking investors, and even crowdfunding. I have used strategic partnerships to raise funds and support my marketing. Having an endorsement and having these partners send out e-mails to their lists about your film will cost you nothing, and you can't usually pay for that type of marketing support.

Another way to fund your project is through sponsorships and paid advertising. There are people who have a service or business who are looking for unique ways to advertise and promote themselves, their work, and/or their books, and they will pay to be in your film.

You don't have to sell out your filmmaking integrity to use this option. You have to be honest about what you intend to say and do with your project, and you have to be clear about what their agenda and desired outcome is. I have used this option multiple times successfully, most recently on a docuseries called *Radical Dating.* I wanted to follow singles as they did a personal-development process around relationships. I approached several of the bigger dating coaches and chose one program I really believed in. I worked with them and found coaches who were aligned with the message and the intent and created a win-win for all of us. I needed funding and had an idea; they wanted exposure, a film of themselves to use for their own promotional materials, and they were filmed by a professional film crew. In the end I got a docuseries and they each got a three-minute trailer/commercial promoting their work. They would most likely pay upward of $5,000 to have that created on their own. This way, they not only got their website video, but they also had an entire series they could promote, pull footage from, and use to generate their own press and marketing materials. Those efforts also supported the marketing of the project as a whole. I wasn't required to pay them back, I owned the copyright on the series, and they owned their footage. Of course, this isn't right for every project, and it's important that you're clear that they are paying for participation. In *Radical Dating,* I held on to final cut, and while they didn't have any say in what I used or didn't use, we had a very clear agreement about what the intent was for the project, how the footage would be used, and that I would not misrepresent them or their work. Because our message was aligned from the beginning, this was not hard to accomplish.

In addition to having people pay to be in your project, you can always offer screen credit/website marketing, etc., to groups, organizations, individuals who supported your project without having them in the film. Remember when TV shows had an ad before them that said, "This program is sponsored by . . ." It all comes down to being clear about your intent and being sure that by aligning with that particular sponsor you are not hurting the integrity of your project or yourself.

PRODUCTION

SECTION IV

OK, YOU'VE GOT YOUR MONEY, or some of your money. It's realistic to assume that you will start your project without having all of the funding figured out. Especially in documentaries, funding comes in phases.

You've hired a lawyer and created your LLC, finalized any business setup you need.

There are three phases to "production." There is preproduction, production, and postproduction. If you're doing a narrative, this usually happens in the order I listed. With documentaries, you can move in and out of each phase as you plan, shoot, edit, plan some more, shoot some more, edit some more—until hopefully you've got what you need to finish your film.

Preproduction is where you want to get your legal ducks in order and plan out your shoot, regardless of what level your funding is at, and get prepared to hit the road and film.

CHAPTER 10

What Are Your Legal Requirements?

As I have stated over and over again, hire a lawyer. I am not a lawyer. I have been around this business long enough to have enough legal wisdom to be dangerous, as they say, and I still always consult with an attorney.

You've most likely hired one to cover all the legal issues around funding your project. You've already created your operating agreement and other LLC documents. If you haven't, do it now! You will also need a lawyer to review any contract you enter into. Some entertainment lawyers will have packages you can purchase that come with multiple template agreements you can use and will cost you less than creating new ones. You can find lots of templates on the internet, do most of the work yourself, and simply hire a lawyer to review your agreements to make sure nothing is amiss.

I like to keep contracts short and simple. They don't need to be Greek—they need to be clear.

For production, key contracts will most likely be your cinematographer, your editor, and your composer (if you are creating any original music). The key element to all of these contracts, regardless of the position, will be your work-for-hire clause. Of course, you will cover how much you'll pay them, what the term of the agreement is, and any other expectations around equipment, deliveries, travel arrangements, screen credit, back-end participation (this is typically only for your key elements and only if they are working for free on a deferred pay, or reduced pay). Don't feel obligated to give everyone a piece of your movie. If someone is providing a significant contribution in time, creativity, partnerships, or money, then you go ahead; otherwise, pay, a screen credit, an IMDb credit, and food are good enough.

Deferred pay is when you agree to pay them at a later date, usually after the film is making money.

What is a work-for-hire clause? It's language that says whatever they contribute, especially in terms of creative elements, ideas, visuals, artwork, music, etc., has been specifically designed for the use in this project and is therefore owned by the LLC.

It looks something like this:

> **Work Made for Hire.** Any work performed by {insert name of contractee} during employment with {insert company name} ("LLC") shall be considered a "Work Made for Hire" as defined in the U.S. Copyright laws and shall be owned by and for the express benefit of LLC for "{insert project title}." In the event it should be established that such work does not qualify as a Work Made for Hire, {insert name of contractee} agrees to and does hereby assign to LLC all of {insert name of contractee} right, title, and interest in such work product including, but not limited to, all copyrights and other proprietary rights.

You can find many variations on this. This should be used in every agreement you enter into.

There is much discussion about hiring people as independent contractors. The easy answer is if you tell them where to show up, when to show up, and provide some of their equipment, and if they don't have a business license or an LLC, they aren't an independent contractor.

The IRS and most states use common law principles to define who is an independent contractor. Those rules are essentially:

- If the worker supplies his or her own equipment, materials, and tools

- If all necessary materials are not supplied by the employer
- If the worker can be discharged at any time and can choose whether or not to come to work without fear of losing employment
- If the worker controls the hours of employment, thus indicating they are acting as an independent contractor
- Whether the work is temporary or permanent

It's likely no one you are working with will qualify under those rules. Even if your editor supplies their own computer and software, they usually need to be considered an employee, unless they have their own LLC or business entity you have contracted with and is billing you. I don't recommend risking it; the fines are high, and it may cause you to lose your LLC or assets.

The good news is that you can contract with a payroll service to handle your payroll, collect employment taxes, deduct taxes, and make your payments for you. And most important, they will have a workman's compensation package, so you don't have to try to buy one on your own. There are several reputable payroll services.

Workman's compensation is insurance most states require you to carry that provides wage replacement benefits to employees injured while working for you. You can purchase it through your payroll service. They will also handle paying your payroll taxes and other required payments. You will need to specify which states you are filming because each state has different requirements. Of course, no one wants to make this easy for you!

You will need to purchase a general liability/production insurance package. This covers you in the event of loss or damage to your equipment or filming locations or if something happens on your set to someone other than an employee. Usually you will be required to have a package that is from $1 million to $3 million general liability. This can be one of your most expensive costs. It's generally calculated based on your budget. You can work with production companies that have a production package who will allow you to buy into theirs for a premium. If you do this, be sure that they have enough coverage and have the ability to list multiple productions on their policy. You should enter into a basic production services agreement with them and then any location agreements or equipment rentals. Basically anyone who requires a certificate of insurance will have to be under their name. This is because they are the entity that is responsible for the rental. They may even have to pay for it from their bank account. Basically, follow the money; the insurance company will, and if they find any instance in which they can find a reason not to pay, they will.

In addition to your crew agreements, you will also need a location agreement and a release for any on-camera talent.

A location agreement covers the use of the location. If you intend to use any signage or identifying marks at the location, make sure this is covered in your agreement. If they have artwork on the walls, make sure it is owned by them and not on loan. Artists can be particularly testy if they see their artwork featured in a film when they were not compensated, and it's incorrect to assume the owner has the rights. If you can, remove any wall hangings or artwork or have it expressly identified in the agreement and that the owner represents they have the rights to it.

Make sure your location agreement covers every space you will be using on and off camera. Do you need special access to an elevator or an extra room to store equipment? Depending on the level of equipment you are using, you may need to pull a permit to film at the location. Are you blocking street access, elevators, or safety exits? I usually stay small when I'm on location and can get away without having to do this. But if you're filming on the street or out in public and you've got more than yourself and a camera, then be advised,that you may be shut down and/or have your gear confiscated if you haven't pulled the proper permits.

It sounds fun to go all guerilla and rogue—until the cops come, that is. I like to know exactly what's required wherever I film, and then if I can avoid some of the costly expenditures, such as permits, I'll skip them. I go by the saying "Know the rules before you break them and weigh the risks." (OK, you did not actually read that.)

Here is an example of a basic location agreement:

LOCATION AGREEMENT FORM

THIS AGREEMENT, effective as of ___ of _____, 20___, is made by and between {YOUR NAME/COMPANY} ("Producer") and {GRANTOR} ("Grantor"), with respect to Producer's use of the location described below on the production of the motion picture currently entitled "{TITLE OF YOUR FILM}" (the "Picture").

1. FILMING LOCATION: For good and valuable consideration, receipt and sufficiency of which is acknowledged, Grantor permits Producer to use the property and the surrounding area, including any signage or identifying materials, located at _____ ("Property") in connection with the Picture for rehearsing, photographing, filming, and recording scenes and sounds for the Picture.

2. PRODUCER'S RIGHTS: Producer may exhibit, advertise, and promote the Picture or any portion thereof whether or not the Property is identified, in any and all media which currently exist or which may exist in the future in all countries, in perpetuity.

3. IDENTIFICATION OF PROPERTY: Producer shall not be required to identify or depict the Property in any particular manner. Grantor acknowledges that any identification of the Property which Producer may furnish shall be at Producer's sole discretion.

4. TIME OF ACCESS: The permission granted hereunder was for the period that commenced on or about _____ and continued until _____. The permission shall also apply to future retakes and/or added scenes, if necessary.

---

5. ALTERATIONS TO LOCATION: Producer represents that any changes on the Property has been returned and restored to its original place and condition, or repaired, if necessary.

6. COMPENSATION: Please check one:
- ☐ Grantor has agreed to allow Producer to use the Property at no charge to Producer.
- ☐ Producer shall provide Grantor with the following compensation: $_____.

7. INDEMNIFICATION: Producer agrees to indemnify and hold harmless Grantor from and against any and all liabilities, damages, and claims of third parties arising from Producer's use of the Property (unless such liabilities, damages, or claims arise from breach of Grantor's warranty as set forth below) and from any physical damage to the Property caused by Producer, or any of its representatives, employees, or agents. Grantor agrees to indemnify and hold harmless Producer from and against any and all claims relating to breach of this Agreement.

8. INSURANCE: Producer agrees to name Grantor and Property address on their General Liability Policy of at least $1 Million.

9. REPRESENTATIONS AND WARRANTIES: Grantor warrants that it has the right to enter this Agreement and to grant the rights herein.

10. RELEASE: Grantor releases and discharges Producer, its employees, agents, licensees, successors, and assigns from any and all claims, demands, or causes of actions that Grantor may have for libel, defamation, invasion of privacy or right of publicity, infringement of copyright, or violation of any other right arising out of or relating to any of the rights granted herein.

11. ARBITRATION: All disputes under this Agreement shall be settled pursuant to binding arbitration under the rules of the

Independent Film and Television Alliance ("IFTA"). The prevailing party will be entitled to reasonable attorney fees and costs.

ACCEPTED AND AGREED:

PRODUCER   GRANTOR

_____   _____

By: _____   By: _____
        (Printed Name)   (Printed Name)

A photo release or talent release is the agreement you will use with any on-screen talent. There is actually a great app called Easy Release that I use. It makes releases like this paperless. They have multiple different templates that you can fill in that cover most on-screen types of situations. You can e-mail them to yourself and your subject instantaneously and print them when you need them. This works for basic interviews with experts, etc.

Here is an example of a video release form:

VIDEO RELEASE FORM

I, _____, hereby grant permission to _____, the rights of my image, in video or still, and of the likeness and sound of my voice as recorded on audio or video tape

☐ with payment of $_____ (US Dollars).
☐ without payment or any other consideration.

I understand that my image may be edited, copied, exhibited, published, or distributed and waive the right to inspect or approve the finished product wherein my likeness appears. Additionally, I waive any right to royalties or other compensation arising or related to the use of my image or recording. I also understand that this material may be used in diverse educational settings within an unrestricted geographic area.

Photographic, audio or video recordings may be used for ANY USE which may include but is not limited to:

- Film, Web Series, or Other Entertainment Media;
- Presentations;
- Courses;
- Online/Internet Videos;
- Media;
- News (Press);

By signing this release, I understand this permission signifies that photographic or video recordings of me may be electronically displayed via the internet or in the public educational setting.

I will be consulted about the use of the photographs or video recording for any purpose other than those listed above.

There is no time limit on the validity of this release nor is there any geographic limitation on where these materials may be distributed.

This release applies to photographic, audio, or video recordings collected as part of the sessions listed on this document only.

By signing this release, I acknowledge that I have completely read and fully understand the above release and agree to be bound thereby. I hereby release any and all claims against any person or organization utilizing this material for educational purposes.

Full Name: _____

Street Address/PO Box: _____

City: _____ State: _____ Zip Code: _____

Phone: _____   Fax: _____

E-mail: _____

Signature: _____   Date: _____

If this release is obtained from a presenter under the age of 19, then the signature of that presenter's parent or legal guardian is also required.

Parent's Signature: _____   Date: _____

If you are creating a film about a specific person, their life events, then you will need a life-rights agreement. This can become extremely detailed, and I would definitely not use an app for that. Life rights can be tricky, as you may only be purchasing the rights to one person's story and not the others involved. How this is negotiated will determine distribution liability (errors-and-omissions insurance) later.

Regarding brands, branded clothing, etc., the best practice is to try to avoid it. Have people wear nondescript clothing and avoid using branded products wherever possible. If you accidentally see a Coke can in the background, you're most likely going to be fine, but if your subject is drinking a Coke while spewing hate filled language, Coke is probably not going to be happy. Use your logic here. I will explain fair use in a later chapter.

If you film on the street or in an area that has people not directed by or under your control, then you must post signage around the perimeter of your filming area notifying them that filming is taking place and by them entering this area they will be filmed. Identify the name of your production and your LLC. Take lots of pictures of your posting so you can show that it was clearly marked in case you run into trouble later.

Errors and Omissions (E&O) insurance: E&O insurance is what most distributors will require in order to show your film anywhere.

Sometimes this can be avoided if you've covered all your bases, have a contract for anything and everything, and can show that you are at a low risk for any lawsuits pertaining to the content of your film. Again, if you have real-life people or talk about real-life people and events when you don't have rights to them, then this will be tough to get.

Honestly, I think E&O insurance is a bit of a racket; you are basically required to prove you won't be sued so you can buy insurance in case you get sued. I have rarely had to buy this because I cover my bases pretty well. You can include an indemnification clause in your distribution agreement (if they will accept it) that essentially says if they get sued, you'll cover for them and that you have the means (i.e., the money) to do so.

There are other negotiations you will deal with, like stock footage, music, and other rights. I will cover those in other chapters.

One last negotiation to mention here—your first. The one you have with your lawyer. Many lawyers will offer up funding opportunities, distribution opportunities, etc., in exchange for some sort of producer credit, a piece of the back end, and a reduced fee. I think this is great. If this happens, hire another lawyer to negotiate your deal with that lawyer.

Remember that you can say no, but you might lose the deal, and if you do, it's probably a good thing.

CHAPTER 11

Your Team

It's my opinion that filmmaking is a collaborative art. You are the leader, the one with the vision and the most invested in your project, and finding the right team members are essential to the success of your film.

You've already done some of this when choosing your lawyer and financiers. They may not seem as if they are part of the art of the endeavor, but they are. Each person you invite onto your team not only has an important role to play in terms of their job or responsibilities, but also, in my opinion, in terms of the energy they bring to the project. Think of it like this. If you bring someone to your team who doesn't fully live up to their commitment, rubs you the wrong way, or has a counterintuitive work style to your own, it will cause you stress and it will cause other team members stress. Each person ultimately impacts everything about the film and whether it has good mojo or icky mojo. So choosing your team members is an important part of the process. Don't wait until you need someone to start immediately to begin your search. Give yourself time to make conscious choices.

For those of you thinking that you'd rather go it alone, I hear you—but I highly recommend not doing this. For sure, there will be times when it's just you, alone in a dark room, editing or writing or watching footage. But having outside support and additional eyes and ears on your project can really enhance it. Having trusted allies to bounce ideas off, to be with you when you do interviews, and to watch rough cuts will not only create a more positive experience, but it will also make your film better.

How do we choose team members? In some cases, it's lifelong friends, fellow students, people who have as much passion about the project as you do. These people are a wonderful asset as long as you have had the tough conversations about everyone's expectations, you are clear on each person's responsibilities and tasks, and you have a very defined working relationship and contract. It's just like I said with someone who might be a friend and an investor. Regardless of how long you've known a potential team member (especially friends and family), having a contract will save that relationship when things get tough—and they will. In every project, there comes a moment of disagreement. When everything is spelled out in a contract prior to the film getting started, it will help alleviate any issues later on.

Your key team members beyond your lawyer and financiers will most likely be a cinematographer, an editor, and a composer, as well as a postproduction producer and, if your film has one, a graphics person. Sometimes the editor can fill all three postproduction roles, and sometimes they can't. Be very clear with everyone about what you expect from them technically. For example, do you expect the film to be shot handheld? Do you expect your editor to do motion graphics and titles? Not everyone is a jack-of-all-trades, even within their own craft, so be specific early on, and if they tell you they can't do it or aren't good at it, believe them. If you try to push someone into to doing something they aren't good at, then you're responsible if it doesn't work out the way you had hoped. Sometimes, the DP or another crew member will tell the leader (i.e., the first AD, the director, or the producer) that it will take twenty minutes to prepare the set or get hair and makeup ready. One thing that has always frustrated me is when the leader responds by saying we don't have that much time and it's somehow the responsibility of the *crew member* to fix the issue in less time. Here's what's wrong with that, in case you can't already see it: no one else is responsible for a leader's lack of planning, and when you don't respect the information given to you by your team, then you either hired the wrong team member or you're not managing them properly. For sure, there are moments when things come up and the time you thought you had becomes shortened. How you work with your team to allow them to deliver on the quality of work you expect from them will directly impact their level of commitment to the project. If you're always pressuring them, not giving them the tools they need or the time, then that's a reflection on *you*, not them.

Before you go about hiring your team, it's important to understand your own leadership style. This will help you choose the right people to support your vision, not argue with it. It will also help you find the people you actually need, and it will help you see ways in which you can improve on your overall leadership style and your communication skills. You may not be aware of how you communicate, and you may be surprised to find out. You may have a few "aha" moments of realizing why maybe things didn't work out so well in other relationships. As you review the different styles of leadership and communication, try not to judge yourself or feel bad if you don't like what you learn. You have the opportunity to change any habits that won't serve you or the success of your film.

Are you a taskmaster and micromanager? Do you want people to do things your way or are you open to allowing people to do things in their own way as long as the end result matches your vision?

Do you prefer to have a more personal relationship with the people you work with (someone to hang out with after a long shoot day, someone you can have a beer or a cup of tea with)? Or are you happy if they just get the job done and go home at the end of the day? Why is this important? Because you may end up traveling with this person and possibly sharing a hotel room! Are they a vegan and you're a meat-and-potatoes kind of person? Things like this may seem petty and silly, and yet they can derail a shoot pretty quickly. If you're going to be traveling with this person and sharing a hotel room, ask them about this. Do they have any quirky habits that might make the arrangement awkward? Like I said, have the tough conversations before you're stuck in a Motel 6 in the middle of nowhere and can't sleep because they snore, loudly.

I once worked with a cinematographer, a woman. I figured we could share a hotel room for our travel. I made an assumption that turned out to be wrong; luckily, it was caught a couple of days before we left, but it did make her uncomfortable that I hadn't asked. I was able to get her an additional hotel room, and it all worked out; however, it cost me a few pennies and some uncomfortable moments that could have easily been avoided.

What is your communication style? Do you like to discuss every detail step-by-step or are you more of a broad approach kind of person?

There are basically four different types of communication styles: passive, aggressive, passive-aggressive, and assertive.

> **Passive:** generally quieter, less verbal, tends to wait for others to speak first. If this is your style, I suggest working with someone to become more assertive prior to embarking on a journey of making a film. Passive communicators tend to end up with their vision being trampled on by more assertive or aggressive communicators. Going with the flow has its advantages, but it's not ideal when you're the leader.

> **Aggressive:** this type of communicator is usually the loudest in the room, demanding and speaking with intense authority. They can be intimidating and a little controlling. If this is your style, practice speaking in a softer voice, slow down, and breathe more. It's OK to have a vision and know what you want, but you just don't want to scare anyone while you express it.

> **Passive-Aggressive:** you tend to have lots of opinions and judgments but don't often share them verbally. You may keep things to yourself until you finally lose your cool. If this is a trait you have, practice learning to share your thoughts and feelings calmly, as they happen. Trust yourself and your instincts, and remember you did the work to bring your team together and they have your back.

Passive-aggressive people can bring down the morale of your entire team, even more so than any other type of communication style. Passive-aggressive people can sow division in your team without you even being aware of it, so be wary of anyone like this, and if this is your style, then do some work to learn how to communicate your thoughts and feelings in a healthy way before you embark on trying to lead a team. This will make a huge difference in the outcome of your film and your life.

Assertive: this is really where you want to be. It's the most effective and positive way to communicate to people, especially as a leader. FYI: *Assertive* doesn't equal *asshole*. You know when to speak and when to listen; you know how to clearly communicate your ideas and your feelings calmly and with respect. You don't blame others, you speak often using "I" statements, you ask genuine questions to gain clarity, and you aren't afraid to be wrong.

Some other things to consider. Are you "The Boss"—an autocratic leader—in charge, and the buck stops with you? Are you more of a democratic leader, listening to all sides and choosing the path that has the most people voting for it? Neither of these in and of themselves makes you a bad leader. We all have multidimensional personalities, and the key to building a successful team is really knowing everyone on it. Their quirks, what makes them tick, what sets them off, how they are best inspired, what their communication style is.

It's your job to know this about yourself first so that you can build a team around you that supports your leadership strengths and weaknesses. We all have a weakness or two (or three). Knowing yours and having the ability to discuss it with potential team members will empower everyone to thrive and create without the stress and anxiety often caused when people who work together haven't spent time examining their shortcomings for themselves.

You're going to become pretty close with these people. You're going to be spending a lot of time with them. They have a life outside of your project—is it stable? Is there anything on their horizon that might impact them and or your film? You don't have to get too personal to determine any of this. You can usually tell by spending some time with them, and it doesn't necessarily mean they aren't right for your project. Going into production aware of as many of the potential pitfalls or issues that may arise and having a backup plan is what will make those issues *non*issues.

Your cinematographer is the closest person to you during production. This person is responsible for capturing your vision on-screen. If you aren't doing this yourself, then finding the right cinematographer as early as possible in the development of your project is important. You're going to want to look at as many reels as possible. A reel is a compilation of footage shot by a cinematographer. Watch entire films they've shot, show them films and images and your look book, and have lots of conversations with them about this prior to hiring them. Talk to others they have worked with in the past and ask questions not only about how the final product turned out, but also about how are they on set. How do they work with other people? What is their communication style? Talk to people who work for them, not just people they've worked *for*. Talk to their last directors and producers. Each of these people may have a different experience in working with them, one more creatively and one more on the business side of things; it's key to know both.

This person is going to be responsible for the visual representation of your film, so take you time in choosing them.

Your editor is who you'll spend more time with in postproduction. However, hiring them as early is possible will help you not only with creating your vision, but also with how you organize your film when you're ready to edit. Just like with your cinematographer, get referrals, talk to people they've worked with, watch their reels and films, and share your vision. How do they listen? How do they communicate and collaborate? What do they think of your ideas and vision? Clearly, if someone hates your ideas, they probably aren't the right choice.

Other team members: As I've shared above, before you hire anyone to work on your project, take the time to really examine all aspects of their working and communication styles in addition to their body of work. Often, we focus more attention on their reels and portfolios than on what it's going to be like to actually work with them. Ask a lot of questions, and be open with them. This project is important to you, and you want to create a positive, productive, and successful working relationship and ultimately a successful film.

On many occasions, I have chosen the seemingly less qualified, less "sexy" résumé over the one with the most IMDb credits. I have always found that when I create a symbiotic team of qualified professionals, with a balance of men and women and personalities, the entire project benefits.

Some interesting generalizations I've experienced with my different team members: not always true, for sure . . .

Sound guys and gals are usually the quiet ones, harder to read, very techie. They have a lot of random stuff in that very small bag they carry. They often feel unheard and ignored and less important (which is often true because everyone always seems to forget about sound, probably because they are so quiet!). Make sure to check if they need anything before every take, and have some sort of signal if something goes awry for them and they need to cut or do something over. Check with them after you cut too.

DPs are usually more emotional and temperamental. Don't rush them. If a DP says it's going to take 15 minutes, then give it to them, or have a good reason why you can't. They are focused on making it look perfect for you, and if you're constantly cutting their time to create "short," they'll start to feel their creativity is diminished and that you don't care about how the shot looks, which is the main reason you hired them.

Remember, your job is not only as a director and or producer, but also as the CEO in charge of morale. This is why I often refer to the producer (and sometimes the director) as "The Mother." Moms run the ship, keep everyone organized, and are ready with a bandage and a hug when someone's knee (or ego) gets bumped.

A note about on-set communication—especially when you are interviewing someone. Set up a code of conduct. For me, I am the only one who directs the subject. Exceptions: when the DP is setting the frame and needs them to move one way or another, or when the sound person needs a sound check. When a retake is needed or an answer must be repeated, my team notifies me with a signal, and I communicate to the subject.

This avoids having too many cooks in the kitchen, which can over-whelm by the subject. You want them to be focused on you and what you are talking about. If too many people are giving them direction, they aren't sure who to listen to.

This doesn't mean no one talks to your subject and they all walk around in silence. Feel the room, act professional, joke if it's appro-priate, don't if it's not. Support the comfort of your subject and the success of your interview.

Think of your team as your film's family. You as the leader are the mother/father figure, but you need some grounded, practical aunts and uncles, and a couple of crazy (the good kind of crazy) ones to make things interesting and fun. You'll also need at least one set of grandparents (I usually think of these as the lawyers and financiers). You're going to have some dysfunctional moments, some upsets, some high times, and definitely some stress. Having a team of peo-ple around you who are conscious, aware, and emotionally intelligent will make a world of difference in your experience of making the film and in the way the film turns out.

CHAPTER 12

How Do I Get What I Want from an Interview?

Before we discuss the art of a good interview, let's explore how we choose whom to interview and in what order.

For most films, the interview subjects present themselves. They are experts, or they are actual participants in the story. There are a couple of ways to approach this, and then there is simple practicality and budget.

If you can, make sure that your most important interview, your main subject or expert, is available to do multiple interviews. I do an initial interview with them and then go out and do corroborating interviews, and I may need to go back to my main subject to clarify something based on what came up in other interviews.

This may be easier said than done, especially if your main subject is hard to get to (i.e., geographically) and if your interviews are spread out around the country or the world and your budget doesn't always allow this. If you've got one shot to film your main subject, at least try to arrange additional Skype/phone interviews. Much can be done with the audio captured from those subsequent conversations. If you do this, make sure your audio quality is as high as possible, so you can use it as voice-over later, and always make sure they are aware you're recording the conversation.

I try to get as many interviews as possible. The more the merrier. Even if I have twenty-five interviews, it's my practice to use only the most important and fully relevant subjects. It can get confusing for your audience to have too many voices and/or people to keep track of in the film. However, having as many options available makes the editing process a whole lot easier. It also informs you better as a filmmaker and can help you avoid any contradictions or misinformation. If you have two subjects with very different views or versions, you can either choose one or explore that contradiction in the film.

Another option is to record a Skype/phone interview with your main subject first, go about filming your other interviews, and save the main subject's actual filming for last. Again, make sure your audio quality is high, and if you can, set up the Skype camera for them in such a way that you could even use that footage if needed. In this option, you can have all your notes ready from your previous interviews and your Skyped conversation with them and be prepared to go deep and get all that you need to cut your film together.

With either option, if time permits, have each interview transcribed immediately and pull your pieces together into a rough cut or a paper cut. (I'll explain these in our chapters on editing.) Doing a rough edit as you work will help you know what questions you must have answered in order to cut the film together.

This isn't always possible when you're doing interviews back-to-back, so copious note-taking and watching interviews as you fly, drive, or travel will help. There is nothing worse than wishing you'd asked a question and having no access to the subject again.

Once you've got your schedule of interviews set and are ready to go, do your research. This should go without saying, but it's important to read every book, explore their social media, google the heck out of them, and write out your list of questions. Sometimes you're going to need to prep your interview subject.

You will, of course, have already had contact with them, and it's good to prepare them with some of the questions you're going to cover. You don't have to give them every question, but some people will require a written set of questions prior to your showing up to film and won't allow you to stray from them. Each individual interview will be different, and if you want the interview to go well, cover all of this prior to the actual shoot day, and respect your agreements.

You might have some gotcha interviews planned. If so, be prepared for what happens when they throw you out, don't show up, or don't give you what you expected. How will this impact your film? Have a couple of backup interviews planned.

If you have questions that people don't want to answer or evidence that what they are saying isn't quite the truth, prepare for how you intend to deal with that.

When you're doing your preinterview, pay attention to how your subject speaks. Do they enunciate? Do they tend to answer questions in long, drawn-out ways? Are the succinct? Too succinct? I recommend some sort of video call prior to your shoot so that you can watch them as they speak. Do they talk with their hands? Do they tend to repeat themselves? Are they nervous? Talk too fast? Too slow? All of this is going to impact how you conduct your interview and how you direct them. Most of the people you are going to interview aren't actors and haven't spent much time in front of a camera, so you're going to need to coach them on how they can best represent themselves and deliver what you need.

What kind of interviewer do you need to be? Soft, gentle, vulnerable? Tough, direct? This is where you need to be the actor and show up in the right way to get what you need.

Be ready to listen and have your questions memorized if you can. If you've done your homework, you won't really need to sit there with a clipboard and a pen. This can be intimidating to your subject, and it can also make you seem less connected to them in person. The best way to interview someone is to make them feel comfortable and as if you're having a conversation where cameras happen to be rolling.

When conducting your interview, ask your subject to incorporate your question into their answer. (This is why asking short, simple questions helps.)

Q: What is your favorite color?
A: My favorite color is blue.

As opposed to:
Q: What is your favorite color?
A: Blue.

It's much easier to edit when what the person is talking about contains context. Don't be shy about asking the question again or reframing the question if you don't get the answer you need. If the person stumbles on a word, wait for them to finish and then ask them to reanswer the question. Make sure they don't feel like they've made a mistake. I find that I need to often reassure my subjects that they are doing great and blame requests on my DP (don't worry, they're used to it . . . it's sort of a thing we do to keep our subjects from getting nervous).

Prep your crew. Just as you need to be prepared, your crew needs to know what is about to happen. Is this interview an ambush? Or is someone about to share their most intimate secrets? The energy on the set will impact how the interview goes. Make sure everyone is aware of any restrictions or specific needs. For example, are you filming in a hospital and can only film or be in certain areas? I once filmed in a prison, and my utility person had a knife in their pocket, which is totally normal for their job but not OK in a prison. Never assume your team knows all of this, and even if they do, have everyone check their pockets, turn off their phones, etc., every time. Remember you are the parent and people can forget, get distracted, or simply just not be aware of what guidelines you set up beforehand.

Most important, listen to your interviews. Let them speak. Make your questions simple and short. Unless you are part of the film, this isn't about showing off how smart you are. It's about allowing your subject to share what you need from them. Don't interrupt them if they stumble or take a moment to think; don't finish their sentences for them. There is nothing worse than being in the edit room and realizing the only usable content is coming from you. Be a good listener, and be prepared to put down your list of questions and follow the interview. Being present—listening and ready to ask a good follow-up question—will make or break your interview. Too often, I see people get so focused on their list of questions, they miss what could have been the best piece of the entire film. Allow your subject to be candid. You've got to follow their lead and make them feel comfortable enough to say what you need them to say. If you overwhelm them with long questions or interject too often, they are going to clam up on you.

This is why your preinterview is important. You will learn what their communication style is, and you'll know where to start the interview and where to end it. You'll know how to show up. Assertive and strong? Soft and gentle? Funny and light? Setting your energy to match theirs and having the ability to bring theirs up if it's too low will help you get the interview you want. Being good at interviewing is sort of like being a therapist. Try to know the psyche of your subject before you interview them.

I realize this isn't always possible. However, you can figure out a person pretty quickly if you haven't spent any time with them prior to your interview. How do they greet you? Hug or handshake? Do they meet your eyes or look away? Learn to read people's body language and find out as much as you can before you get into the room with them.

If you're interviewing a woman and you have money in your budget, hire a makeup and hair person. This may seem extravagant. However, in my experience, when a woman feels comfortable and like she looks good, she won't worry so much about it and can be more focused on the interview itself. All this may sound horribly chauvinistic, and I'm not saying women are vain. Some women couldn't care less, but I have found that asking if they'd prefer that and offering it up makes a huge difference. Another tip: if you're an all-male crew and you're interviewing a woman, have another woman on the set when the interviewee is there. Some women are not comfortable in all-male settings; your interviewee needs to feel safe and welcome if you want to get good footage. As a sign of reciprocation, if you're an all-female crew and you're interviewing a man, I say have a man on the set. Again, this isn't some gender-sexist perspective; it's practical. It's an awareness about humans and how we work. Some people won't care who's on set; your job is to be prepared and to create an environment that is best suited to getting the footage you need. This is the psychology of producing your film. It's your job to do whatever it takes to create the environment needed to get the interview you want. I am always focused on using my intuition and creating an environment where people feel comfortable and safe, especially since it's likely the person I am interviewing isn't used to cameras and lights. I might even be in their home or office, their personal space, and they are probably sharing something deeply personal. Even if they are a specialist or an expert, the more comfortable you make them, the less likely you'll be to end up with canned responses, which can come off as dry and boring on film.

All of this can be figured out prior to your actual shoot; the more you are prepared, the better your interview will be. You've got your crew and your gear, and you've maybe flown halfway around the world. Don't skimp of the psychological aspect of your shoot.

People often ask me how long an interview takes. It takes as long as it takes to get what you need, or as much time as you have been allotted with the subject. If you're prepared, then I don't recommend eight- to ten-hour interviews, unless you really need all that footage. Remember, you're going to have to watch and edit all of this footage. Get as much time as you need and a little bit extra.

Do you need to film inserts of family photos? Are their specific shots you need in order to tell your story?

Leave time in your day for B-roll (supplemental footage used as cutaway over voice-over). Do you want to film your subject looking at family photos? Do you want them to walk in the park? What else do you need from them in order to tell your story without having the camera on their face the entire time? Besides their telling of the story, what compelling and unique footage can you film with them that you can use to show their perspective?

I always try to get digital images of photos, if available, or any other documents that I may need to show. This is something you should prepare your subject for prior to your getting there. Hopefully, they will have everything ready for you.

On the technical side of your interview, you've already decided on your look and feel for the film. Deciding where to do your interviews is as important as the actual interview. Filming them in the environment that best suits your look and their story is best. Do you want all of the interviews to look the same? Book a soundstage or black-box theater. I am not a big fan of green screen; however, for some projects it works, especially if you intend to use a lot of motion graphics or text backgrounds. You can purchase a green-screen kit to travel with you, which helps. Be sure your DP knows how to light a green screen and that you have enough space to use it. Make sure wherever you film, you know you have access to power and what the light is like. (When is sunset? Will the windows require blocking or can you use that light?) If I'm filming in a subject's home or office, I ask them to send me pictures of the space, so I can be sure I have what I need before I get there. Ask them about sound. What day does the gardener come? You definitely don't want to book your interview on that day or the day when their neighbor's gardener comes. Is there an airport or a highway nearby? Do they have a barking dog in their house or close by? Can the air-conditioning or heating (or even the refrigerator if it's a loud one) be turned off for the duration of the shoot? Too often we forget about these seemingly minor issues that could affect sound quality until it's too late. Be sure to investigate all potential obstacles to getting what you need. If you can, have a tech scout (a meeting with your DP, lighting crew, or other team members) at the location several days before you shoot to review all these questions. Where will you park? How do you get the equipment inside? Are you filming outside? Did anyone check the weather? I know I may seem like a nagging mom—I am, actually. Should any one of these issues pop up at your shoot, it could derail the whole day, and I don't know anyone who can afford that.

CHAPTER 13

B-Roll and Other Cool Stuff That Makes Your Film a Film

If you watch most documentaries, they aren't wall-to-wall talking heads. Films move with images, animations, and action shots that further the story along.

Besides B-roll, there is animation, graphics, and reenactments.

Let's start with B-roll.

There are different kinds of B-roll. There is the B-roll you film yourself, there is B-roll you buy, and then there is B-roll you use via fair use.

As I mentioned in the last chapter, you can plan to shoot B-roll while you're shooting your interviews. Having footage of your subjects in their daily lives, driving, cooking, gardening, or hiding a murder weapon are all great ways for your audience to fully connect with the subject. It helps people connect with them emotionally and learn more about them without always having to look at the same few angles in your face-to-face interview. It also gives the viewer time to integrate information, breathe, and contemplate. B-roll can be used with voice-over or montages with music or as opening, transitional, or act endings. It's also a wonderful tool if you are filming subjects doing something specific to the story. Are they an artist? Film them creating their art, film them in their office, or doing their job. The point is to have visually interesting and relevant footage that you can cut away to in your film.

You can also purchase stock footage from literally thousands of sites and even footage from TV shows and films or footage in which someone owns the copyright. You may not be able to jet over to Dubai for that skyscape shot at dusk you would like to open your film with. You may want to use a clip from *Seinfeld* or *Home Alone 2*. Someone usually owns the copyright, unless it's fallen into public domain. Public domain is when a piece of work has exhausted its copyright term and is now available for use without any contract or written approval.

What is a copyright?

A copyright is a legal type of protection grounded in the U.S. Constitution and granted by law for the original works of authorship fixed in a tangible medium of expression (i.e., literary, dramatic, musical, and artistic works, such as poetry, novels, movies, songs, computer software, and architecture). It doesn't matter whether it's been published or not. Copyright does not protect facts, ideas, systems, or methods of operation, or recipes even, although it may protect the way these things are expressed.

How is a copyright different from a patent or a trademark?

Copyright protects original works of authorship, while a patent protects inventions or discoveries. Ideas and discoveries are not protected by the copyright law, although the way in which they are expressed may be (e.g., made into a film, written as a book, etc.). A trademark protects words, phrases, symbols, or designs identifying the source of the goods or services of one party and distinguishing them from those of others.

Be careful with trademarks: not only do you have to purchase them for different categories, but you also have to use them or someone else can still use it and claim your trademark was dormant. It's usually not worth it to trademark a logo or the name of a documentary or film unless it's related to a brand or a product being marketed. In that case, trademark the brand or product, not your film.

Why would you purchase a piece of footage instead of just using it and hoping to claim fair use?

Well, you could probably get away with it. However, if it seems that clip from *Seinfeld* is somehow endorsing or making a libelous statement about something in your film, you may have trouble getting past the E&O insurer with your distributor. Or you may just piss of Jerry Seinfeld, and he has deep pockets for litigation.

What is fair use?

Basically, fair use is any use of copyrighted material done for a limited and "transformative" purpose, such as to comment upon, criticize, or parody a copyrighted work. Such uses can be done without permission from the copyright owner.

To read everything you need to know about fair use, check out this site, which will provide you with a pdf that fully explains and explores all aspects of fair use.

> Statement of Best Practices by the Center for Media and
> Social Impact: https://cmsimpact.org/resource/documentarians
> -fair-use-and-best-practices/

When I'm determining if something I'm using falls under fair use, I often reference Ron Dawson's article "The Ultimate Guide to Fair Use and Copyrights for Filmmakers."[9] He nails it. Technically I'm claiming fair use by using some of the quotes from his article, and I am attributing them to him. Since I'm praising his genius at explaining something that can be confusing, mind-numbing, and stressful, I think he'll be OK with it:

> Fair use is a legal doctrine that promotes freedom of expression by permitting the unlicensed use of copyright-protected works in certain circumstances. Section 107 of the Copyright Act provides the statutory framework for determining whether something is a fair use and identifies certain types of uses—such as criticism, comment, news reporting, teaching, scholarship, and research—as

---

9   Ron Dawson, "The Ultimate Guide to Fair Use and Copyrights for Filmmakers," Frame. io Insider, accessed April 29, 2019, https://blog.frame.io/2017/08/30/copyrights-and-fair-use-for-filmmakers/.

examples of activities that may qualify as fair use. Section 107 calls for consideration of the following four factors in evaluating a question of fair use:

1. **Purpose and character of the use,** including whether the use is of a commercial nature or is for nonprofit educational purposes. {. . .}
2. **Nature of the copyrighted work.** {. . .} (Using parts of something more creative in nature, like a movie or book, has a weaker "fair use" argument than news footage or a technical article.)
3. **Amount and substantiality of the portion used in relation to the copyrighted work as a whole.** {. . .} (I.e., Do you *really* need three whole minutes of *Avengers: Age of Ultron* in that video essay about superhero movies? Or will three seconds do?)
4. **Effect of the use upon the potential market for or value of the copyrighted work.** (Will the use hurt the original copyright holder's ability to make money from the work that was copied?)[10, 11]

You may have read that and thought, *Huh?* Fair use is slippery. It looks as if it's very clear, and yet it isn't, and unless you get sued, you may not know if you're doing it right or not. Again, if you think you're going to get sued, you probably will, so check with a lawyer!

I always follow my own set of criteria here.

1. **Is it "transformative"?** How am I using the footage? Am I repurposing it for use in a way that is different from the original intent? This is what it means to be transformative. Are you using a clip from *Charlie and the Chocolate Factory* of Augustus overeating as an example of gluttony

---

10   Ron Dawson, "The Ultimate Guide to Fair Use and Copyrights for Filmmakers."
11   In his article, Dawson cites the following source for his definition of fair use, as well as the list of factors, however the text in parentheses are his own commentary: "More Information on Fair Use," Copyright.gov, accessed April 29, 2019, https://www.copyright.gov/fair-use/more-info.html.

in the modern age? That's educational and probably OK. You could even create a montage of famous overeating shots from movies to show the rate of increased cases of diabetes and obesity and still be good, but if you're making a narrative about an overweight kid and you use that shot in your film, you're probably going to get sued. Even if the overweight kid is watching *Charlie and Chocolate Factory* on a TV in the background, you're more likely to get sued. Documentaries (usually considered educational or newsworthy) have much more leeway when it comes to fair use.

2. **Am I using it to illustrate an argument or point?** There are four uses of copyrighted material that are usually good to go: commentary, criticism, education, and news. Which is why satire, parody, video essays, and documentaries are usually protected by fair use. I say *usually* because I make sure that if I'm using a clip as an example of wrongdoing or negligence or making a claim, I'd best be able to back it up and make sure *not* to make it look as though the creator of the original clip agrees with me.

3. **Am I making an historical point?** Commentary on cultural or political issues? Probably OK.

4. **How long is my clip?** Use no more than ten to fifteen seconds if possible and definitely no more than thirty seconds.

And here's a little reminder from Ron Dawson:

Remember, fair use is the kind of law wherein a transgression isn't definitively determined until after the fact (i.e., you get sued). It's not like running a red light or shooting a person in cold blood, acts which you know beyond a shadow of a doubt beforehand are illegal. So, every time you create media and invoke "fair use," you are technically opening yourself up to litigation if there are no expressed licenses in place. That's just a cold hard truth.[12]

Tell it, Ron . . .

I've seen entire films with "borrowed clips." A great example of this is a doc by one of my dear friends, Patrick Takaya Solomon, called *Finding Joe*. Patrick used clips from every film that followed Joseph Campbell's *The Hero's Journey*. We're talking big chunks—and he totally got away with it. He even got away with clips from *Star Wars!*

Films like *Super Size Me* are considered educational and social commentary, and while McDonald's may not have liked what he had to say in his film, they couldn't really dispute it or claim libel since he was pretty accurate with his facts. McDonald's really couldn't do much of anything.

Companies have sued and lost when convicted murderers are shown drinking Coca-Cola or when people in a nightclub are dancing to their song and something negative goes down. For the most part, if you're filming in a public place and there is music playing, signage, or even people, as long as you've clearly marked that you're filming in the area or can show that the capture of the people, logos, music was incidental, you're going to be fine.

If you want to do a time-lapse shot of Times Square, the huge billboards and advertisements are a part of that classic tourist destination, which clearly identifies New York City. As long as you don't open your shot specifically on a particular ad and they simply appear, then you're good to go.

Here's what you need to know. If you use it, do your research and read up on all the appropriate ways to claim fair use. This topic could literally be a book on its own. Places like YouTube, Vimeo, and the like are usually protected by the DMCA (a law passed in 1998 that essentially protects third-party platforms from being held liable if you use footage you shouldn't have). However, they can and often do

---

12 Ron Dawson, "The Ultimate Guide to Fair Use and Copyrights for Filmmakers."

make you take it down, and they are particularly good at tracking down copyrighted music.

A final thought on fair use: I use it all the time. So far, I've been fine (knock on wood), and it's saved me thousands and thousands of dollars in fees I probably couldn't pay.

In my end credits, I try to give credit to every clip I've pulled. I also include a short fair-use disclaimer just in case:

Fair Use Act Disclaimer
The use of copyrighted material in this film is for educational and or commentary and critique only.

Fair Use
Copyright Disclaimer under section 107 of the Copyright Act of 1976, allowance is made for "fair use" for purposes such as criticism, comment, news reporting, teaching, scholarship, education, and research. Fair use is a use permitted by copyright statute that might otherwise be infringing.

Fair Use Definition
Fair use is a doctrine in United States copyright law that allows limited use of copyrighted material without requiring permission from the rights holders, such as commentary, criticism, news reporting, research, teaching, or scholarship. It provides for the legal, non-licensed citation or incorporation of copyrighted material in another author's work under a four-factor balancing test.

And, especially if the B-roll shot is some sort of a time-lapse or establishing shot, I really try to pay the person who created it. They are mostly starving filmmakers who would really appreciate your fifty bucks.

When you do purchase footage, be sure to select the appropriate rights use when signing the agreement. Sometimes you can purchase the use in stages. Perhaps you're going to do film festivals first. Then select just those rights. If you're only releasing your film in the United States, then only choose domestic rights. If you're going to release it on the web or theatrically, and especially if you are going to profit from it, then purchase worldwide, all rights, in perpetuity. Most websites where you would purchase these shots have a set contract, and you just click the boxes at checkout.

In addition to B-roll, you may want to create animation or graphics of your own. These days it seems as if everyone is a graphic artist and an expert in after-effects. There are tons of prefab creations on sites like Viddyoze, Fiverr, and other trade sites where you can contract someone to inexpensively create just about anything. Just be prepared to not always get that million-dollar look. I love to work with students who are really amazing and, well, let's face it, cheap. They need the work and the experience and the credit.

Have a storyboard created, either by you or have them create one first, and once that's approved, have them start the work. Spend as much time planning the shots as you can before you send them off to do the hard labor; this will save you tons of time and money. Be specific. What fonts do you like? What is the color palette? Should the animation be 2-D or 3-D? Have examples of what you want. The clearer you are in explaining your vision, the better the results will be, especially with someone creating visuals.

Reenactments are fun and have become incredibly popular, but they can be pricey, so I wouldn't attempt them unless you have the budget to really pull it off. If you're doing a documentary about a specific Civil War battle and you don't have the money to make sure every piece of clothing or prop is spot-on, skip it. Your audience will call that out in an instant and you'll lose your credibility.

Filmmaker credibility is your most important asset as a storyteller. Don't skimp or cheat on any of your footage, especially your B-roll or animations. If you can't do it well, don't do it. If you can't find the right shot from the right time period, don't try to pull one over on your audience. Documentary watchers are usually educated in the subject to some degree, and if they can find holes in your story, they will. Once that happens, getting them back into the film is nearly impossible.

Besides music, B-roll (or anything you cut away to) sets the tone and tempo of your film. Use it wisely! Use it to create space between the talking heads, the words, and the information your viewer has to take in and digest. Don't overwhelm the viewer with graphs and text unless it's really important. Choose a style and stick with it, or choose a couple and use them like dance partners. Some filmmakers choose the music first and then find the footage to match; for others, it's the other way around. Either way, they both work together to infuse your audience with the emotional connection to the film.

POSTPRODUCTION

SECTION V

AS I MENTIONED EARLIER, it is often said that films are made at least three times: once in preproduction/planning (the dreaming stage), once while filming (what actually happens, or the doing stage), and once in the editing room (making sense of what you have on film, or the forming perspective/voice stage). I have often found that the film I set out to make isn't the film I ended up with at all, and that's OK. Sometimes it's exactly what I expected. Now is the time to be open to what you see on film. Sometimes that amazing sound bite doesn't look so good once you watch it again—there was a fly on the subject's nose, they stumbled, or they said "um" too much. How do we listen to our film instead of trying to force the film to be what it isn't? Your footage will be your guide. You can make up for missing pieces with B-roll and voice-over, but ultimately what you have in the "can" is your best starting point.

CHAPTER 14

Putting All the Pieces Together to Tell a Compelling Story

By now, hopefully you've had an editor working on some sort of rough cut. Prior to filming, you've met with your editor, and together you have created a basic outline of what should happen in each act. Earlier I shared the hero's journey with you. Here is a basic outline of the three-act structure for any good story—again, just because you're making a doc, even something about the rise of high cholesterol in America, you've got to have compelling story.

A basic three-act structure looks like this:

Basic Three-Act Structure

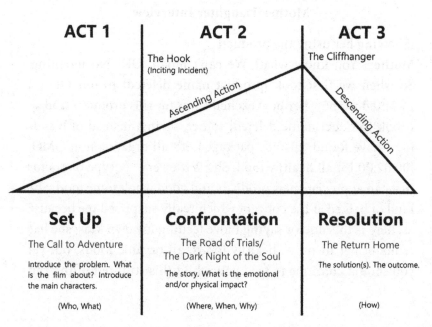

ACT 1	ACT 2	ACT 3
	The Hook (Inciting Incident)	The Cliffhanger
Set Up	**Confrontation**	**Resolution**
The Call to Adventure	The Road of Trials/ The Dark Night of the Soul	The Return Home
Introduce the problem. What is the film about? Introduce the main characters.	The story. What is the emotional and/or physical impact?	The solution(s). The outcome.
(Who, What)	(Where, When, Why)	(How)

As you've been filming, hopefully you've had a chance to watch your footage and pull clips from your transcripts.

I call this your draft paper cut. A paper cut is when you put all the pieces from interviews that you want on to paper. The first draft doesn't have to be in order, and it can have more than one option for each point. I like to have at least three choices, especially if it's an important story point. It's also helpful if you have more than one person saying the same thing, so you can intercut the footage or show it back-to-back to reinforce what you're saying. When I am pulling clips, I highlight the section I want, making sure to pull the time code, and then I put a category/keyword after the clip so my editor can drop everything into bins that can be pulled from when roughing out the first cut.

What is a bin? It's basically a folder in which you drop all the clips that relate to that topic. You could put clips in multiple folders; this is how I organize my clips. Your editor may have a different system, but regardless of what that system is, make sure you both understand it and plan how you will organize your footage ahead of time.

It looks something like this:

Mother/Daughter Interview

{Showing her using the product}

Mother: You know what? We can't moan, OK? No moaning. So when we first took {product name deleted} to our GI . . . I wanted to show her how excited I was for this product. And so I took {product name deleted} to her, saying, instead of blending I have found this; it's packaged, it's all organic, non GMO, {00:02:00.15} all healthy food. She is the very . . . type of doctor that can appreciate new products and good wholesome food. She kind of balked at the concept which really surprised me because . . . here is this doctor saying I love feeding my own kids; she has twins of her own . . . healthy foods, all organic foods, but yet you should continue to feed your child this stuff out of the can

> with corn syrup. It really surprised me. **\<Bins – Act 3 – finding a solution – sharing with others – B-roll product usage\>** But over the months that passed I wore her down and now I am thrilled to say she is now recommending {product name deleted} and {product name deleted} to other families as well. I feel thankful that she was willing to . . . start using the product as well.

I've highlighted the piece I want, and I've stated where it lands, for now. It might change, or I might use something else, but pulling these clips will give your editor a place to start. For the first pass of my paper cut, I usually leave them in the actual transcripts and I ask my editor to read them as well. Who knows? They might find something I've missed. Then either they or I can put them into a document on their own for easier tracking.

I break everything out into acts and then try and put them in the order I want. For example:

Act 1
Bin: B-roll using footage (and so on, you'll probably have
    more than one bin in each act)
Clip #
Clip #
Clip #

Act 2
Clip #
Clip #
Clip #

Act 3
Clip #
Clip #
Clip #

And so on.

Once all the potential pieces you want to use are organized into acts and bins, you can begin the process of selecting the best takes, angles, and clips to tell your story. Some people skip the rest of the "writing process," and do it in the edit. This is my preferred method. To me, there is a huge difference between what reads well on paper and what looks good on the screen. I always choose as many options I can for each point I want to make. But I prefer to work in the edit and not on paper from this point on. This is a personal preference, one that you and your editor should figure out way before you get to this point.

Once you've laid out your rough cut and are happy with your interview pulls, then you can decide what's missing: B-roll, animations, a narrator?

Choosing to use a narrator and deciding what type of voice to use is key. Do you need a strong masculine voice that is assertive and commanding? Do you want a softer, vulnerable voice that brings up emotion? Man or woman? This is an important choice because this voice is essentially your "Voice of God," the all-knowing expositional translator of everything you're missing from other options in your film, like your interviews or your other footage.

To pick a celebrity narrator or not? If you have access to a celebrity who is willing to not only do the narration, but also to help promote the film and use their clout to get the film out into the world, then it's worth it. If they won't, it's not. It's really as simple as that. Some say that a celebrity will help you get a distribution deal, both foreign and domestic. It might, but if paying them takes a significant amount of your budget, which affects your ability to make an overall better film, then it's really not worth it. If you do decide to use a celebrity narrator, be sure to check with the Screen Actors Guild (SAG) and file the appropriate paperwork in order for them to legitimately work on your project. Most celebrities are union members and have restrictions on what they can and can't do, and it's usually required that their projects be union. You can get waivers and sign agreements only if they fall under the SAG agreement, so it's best to get this cleared prior to having a celebrity voice the project.

If you are using narration, you'll need to create a script for your narrator. It's good to have the film available for them to watch as they read, so they can get the timing right.

I use this format when working with narrators:

Documentary Pre- and Post-Script

Topic: The relationship between the arts and a student's success

Creators: Samantha Chang and Emi Kanda

Claim: The arts (drawing, dance, music, acting, etc.) help a person become successful physically, mentally, and academically. The arts essentially teach a child all the important skills in life.

Narration	Visuals	Sounds
Even if it doesn't seem like it, the arts help people, especially students, become successful in life skills. Ninety-five percent believe that the arts teach creativity, expression, and individualism.	images and video of children making art, dancing, acting, etc.	children laughing, teacher explaining something
	someone on a stage (spotlight?)	singing
Eighty-nine percent say the arts are important enough that they need to be included in school curriculum.	someone sitting on the curb, drawing with chalk *OR* art on a student schedule	footsteps, school hallway noises
Ninety-six percent think the arts belong to everyone, not just the fortunate or privileged.	images of the homeless (possibly pictures of the orphans' drawing from Ghana?)	

What if you're going it alone, editing by yourself? This process still stands, but you're just going to have to figure out your own workflow. I have found that the more time I spend away from the footage, the more that I forget that I have. Maybe this is because I'm old and forgetful, but if you're editing alone, then please pay a transcriber and have your footage transcribed immediately after you film it. Review it within five days and pull your choices. You will be glad you did this when you finally make your way behind the computer to edit.

This is where most people get lost. They don't have a plan or a workflow. Just like you planned out your shoot, you must plan out your postproduction process. Do you want to work from the beginning and just keep moving forward? Do you have specific sections you want to tackle first? Remember, one change to Act 3 can impact something in Act 1, so be organized. Having your outline printed and at the ready can help. Make sure you're on track and don't get lost in the weeds. You may have to "kill that baby." OK, I know that phrase sounds horrible, but the expression means that sometimes we fall in love with certain moments or clips and yet they don't fit the overall message or impact we desire, so we have to let them go.

Until you've decided that you're done, play with music and "borrowed footage" for B-roll. Don't be afraid to try things out, screen it, and have it suck. . . . Sucking is where opportunity lies, but only if you can get beyond your ego and your feelings enough to allow the audience to tell you what works.

One of the biggest mistakes that filmmakers make, at least in my opinion, is making a film they "like" and forgetting that film is an art form appreciated by others, interpreted by others and for others.

If you hide your film from others until "you're done" you might not create the outcome you desire.

I like to screen my film in multiple stages. If you can, screen it with people who understand the process. If you can't, then create a short questionnaire and prep your audience. "The sound is bad, the edit isn't final, and I'm looking for specific answers."

Some questions you might ask are:

- What did you learn?
- What did you feel?
- What bothered you?
- Can you tell me about the story you saw?
- What was your favorite moment and why?
- What questions were left unanswered?

These basic questions will help you find the holes. I know, you're smarter than that . . . and yet every time I have braved a screening of an unfinished film, I have learned something. If I end up arguing with more than one person over my story, they won, not me, and it's time to go back into the editing room.

A budgeting trick—budget for reshoots and additional footage. The worst that will happen is that you'll need it. The best is that you won't spend it on reshoots and you can put those remaining funds into your marketing budget—no harm no foul.

You will know in the edit bay whether or not you planned well. I have found time and time again, the more I dream it, the more I plan it, the more risks I take, and the more I listen and allow, the more footage I have to play with when I'm editing, and that is what you want.

I am about to contradict myself, and perhaps it's because after thirty years I've learned to know when to shoot, shoot, shoot and when to save my money. It's because prior to starting, I've dreamed it. I have laid out each beat I need to hit, and I make sure, no matter where I'm at, whom I am interviewing, or what animations or B-roll I am creating, I can tell that story.

That means really understanding the structure of a story, the beats I need to enable an emotional reaction as well as to provide all the necessary exposition. Making a chart not unlike the hero's journey (or the three-act structure) and being certain that I have at least one interview that will fulfill that beat ensures I will end up with a film.

And then I let that all go, trust my instincts and my team, and go for it.

Your editing process will take longer than you expected if you're doing it right. So plan for this in the beginning. In every schedule I create, I add two weeks to every stage. For development, I add two months because it always takes longer for the money to hit the bank than you expect. During production, I leave space for reshoots and additional interviews. (Add a narrator to your budget even if you think you won't be using one.) Postproduction will take you at least a month longer than you hoped, even if you don't have to raise post funds.

If you recall, when I discussed crowdfunding, I mentioned that postproduction is another phase in which to raise funds. While editing, try to create at least one trailer and one teaser. This will help you if you need to raise funds or as you begin your sales process. It's also a great guidepost to make sure your film is on track. Your trailer is a mini version of your film. It must have three acts, tell a story, and be impactful, compelling, and emotional. It must also tell the viewer what to expect. If your film isn't a comedy, then don't make a comedic trailer. Don't get too clever and cute. People want to know what they are committing to. A trailer is typically two to three minutes long, and a teaser can be thirty seconds to one minute. While a trailer or a teaser should be artistic and reflect the look and feel of the entire film, this is a sales piece. Its job is to sell people on the idea of seeing your film.

A basic structure for your trailer is as follows:

1. An introduction of the main idea or quest.
2. An introduction of the main characters/plot.
3. A taste of the emotional experience: funny, scary, insightful?
4. A wrap-up—the call to action. Why should viewers see this film?

Some festivals accept rough cuts. Look at where you are in the editing process: can you enter film festivals now and be finished by their deadline? Even though film festivals accept rough cuts, you should still do your best to provide as complete a film as you can. You can use temporary music and effects. Don't enter a film without these things.

If you have a producer, this is what they'll be focusing on. If not, then you have to do both. The time between finishing your film and selling it will feel like an eternity.

Postproduction consists of more than just editing your film. There are multiple steps to completing and delivering your film. If you've presold your film, you will have received a delivery list. These are

TITLE: _____

Contact _____

SCHEDULE OF DELIVERY MATERIALS

TITLES CANNOT BE SCHEDULED FOR RELEASE UNTIL ALL ITEMS ARE RECEIVED

WHITE TYPE ITEMS ARE 1ST PRIORITY FOR DELIVERY

		Date Due	Date Received
SECTION 1 - FEATURE	1.1 Video Master Pro Res HQ File		
	1.2 Closed Captions		
	1.3 Final Screenplay / Shooting Script (If Available)		
	1.4 DVD Screener or H264 file (preferred)		

SECTION 2 - TRAILER	2.1 Pro Res HQ File		

	3.1 Social Media (if available)		
	3.2 Photos / Stills		
	3.3 Electronic Press Kit (EPK) & Publicity Stills (if available)		
	3.4 Art Files (Key Art)		
	a. 1400W x 2100H		
	b. 548W x 800H		
	c. 1296W x 720H		
	d. 2048W x 768H		
SECTION 3	3.4A DVD Packaging Art		
MARKETING MATERIALS	3.4B DVD Disc Art		
(3.2, 3.4 & 3.6 mandatory	3.5 Press Kit (if available)		
all other as available)	3.6 Long Synopsis (1250 Characters includes spaces)		
	Short Synopsis (240 characters includes spaces)		
	3.7 Biographies (if available)		
	3.8 Special Features (if available)		

1

TITLE: _____ 0

		Date Received
	4.1 Billing block	
	4.2 Paid Advertising Statement (Template)	
SECTION 4	4.3 Chain of Title	
DOCUMENTS	4.4. Music Cue Sheets (Template)	
(Mandatory)	4.5 Errors and Ommisions Insurance Certificate	
	4.6 Stock Footage / Film Clips Clearance	
	4.7 Copyright Notice	

SECTION 5	5.1 Short Form Assignment (Template)		
RESIDUAL	5.2 Certificate of Origin		
DOCUMENTS	5.3 Documentation from Guilds and Unions (if applicable)		
5.1 & 5.2 Mandatory	5.4 Compliance Certificate (if applicable)		

SECTION 6			
FOREIGN OR REGIONAL	Subtitle file(s) (only required if film or portions are not in English)		
LANGUAGE REQUIREMENTS			

SECTION 7			
METADATA	(see Metadata Spreadsheet)		

CONTRACT		

elements required by the distributor. On page 123, you'll find a general list of delivery items you will need. Keep in mind that it can be different depending on the platform. It's best to review updated lists from any platform or distributor you may be working with as early as possible so that you can begin to prepare these items and budget for them. In addition to domestic delivery items, foreign distribution requires additional items, such as textless backgrounds and sound and music cue sheets so they can translate the film into the required language.

Preparing these items can seem overwhelming, especially if you don't know what they are. Even if you can budget for a postproduction supervisor to help you gather everything, it may seem like a silly expense. After going through QC (quality control) and being bumped a few times, you'll see why it's worth it.

CHAPTER 15

All That Other Stuff

Speaking of all that stuff on your delivery list: just because you've edited your film doesn't mean it's finished. There is music, sound design, color correction, B-roll, stock footage, music licensing, and on and on. How do we accomplish all this and get our film done?

Let's start by determining where your film is going to land. If you're going straight to Vimeo or YouTube or some other web platform, you probably don't have to spend a bunch of money on a sound mix or color correction. If you intend to release your film theatrically or on the big screen, taking the time to make sure your film looks good and sounds good in a theater is important. If you intend to release theatrically and you are new to the postproduction process, hire a postproduction supervisor to walk you through delivery. Figuring out all the steps to get your film ready can be overwhelming and costly if you aren't sure what to do or how to do it.

After you've locked picture (i.e., you will not be making any additional changes to the edit), you can begin working on the final elements of your film. You have already begun working with your composer, but they won't do the final score until the picture is locked. For some, having an original score is too expensive, and you can definitely work with websites that have thousands of musical pieces available. You could purchase a music library, which offers you a worldwide all rights license to use whatever music is in the library.

I have found that working with a composer is not as expensive as one might think, and you'll own the music, or at least you have all the rights you need, which gives you much more creative control over the music in your film.

MUSIC LICENSING

Music licensing is a complicated world. There are different types of licenses depending on the use. If you intend to license multiple songs from multiple artists, hire a music supervisor. If you can't afford one, most labels have a department that handles licensing, and they can help you though the process.

You first need to determine who owns the song in question. To do this, search the song title, writer, or publisher (usually listed wherever you can buy the song, for example, iTunes, etc.), then go to BMI or ASCAP. Usually one of these places will provide you with a contact person at the label to begin your inquiry. If you have a relationship with the artist, you can also start there; however, they don't always own all the rights to their song, and you may still have to deal with the label or copyright holder. Just because an artist sings a song doesn't mean they wrote it, and often even if they wrote it, the rights may be held by their label or another publishing company.

There are two rights to every song, publishing rights (the person who wrote the song) and sync rights (the person who recorded it). You will need permission from both to use any song in your film.

After you have figured out who owns what, you'll need to request permission from every party involved. This can get tricky, especially if there are multiple songwriters. The average song may have up to four different writers and as many as six publishers. If you can't get permission from all of them, it's a no-go.

So to be clear, you will need both a publisher license and a sync license.

You will also need to determine what rights you need. This is called "term of use"—where and how are you going to use it?

These rights are essentially the same if you are purchasing rights for music, B-roll images, or anything you use in your film that is held by a copyright holder.

If you are buying from a website such as iStock, you can usually purchase their standard license, which covers everything you need to release the film in theaters. This is the same if you use a music site such as Audioblocks.

For other sites or purchases you will either need:

- Festival rights: allows you to use the song (stock footage, etc.) only in film festivals.
- Domestic theatrical: allows you to release in the United States in theaters.
- Worldwide rights: allows you to release on all platforms in any country.

You always want to set the term length at "in perpetuity," which means forever.

COLOR CORRECTION

Color correction is what you do to make your film look seamless and stylized from shot to shot. It's the process used to enhance the color of your film, also referred to as color grading. You can also add some effects. Do you want your film to look as if it were shot on film or have the colors pop in a specific way? This is where you can correct some lighting issues, skin tone, etc. You want someone who knows what they are doing to do this process for you. It can make or break how your film looks and how the film is perceived.

SOUND MIXING

Sound mixing is another area that matters, especially if you are releasing in theaters. A bad mix can ruin a film. This is typically done on a mixing stage, where you bring all the audio elements of your film together with picture and work to balance the levels, add sound effects, fix audio issues, etc. If you're not releasing in theaters, it's still important to do this process with someone who has an ear for sound.

If you're releasing in theaters, you want to try to get the best sound quality you can. Most use Dolby, and most sound-mixing facilities will assist you in getting the license you need.

In the old days, a film was delivered on a print; nowadays, theaters require a digital delivery. Most theaters are now using satellite to play films. This is great because you don't have to pay upward of $1,000 per print, but now you will usually need a digital cinema package (DCP), which holds your film in a format almost any theater can play it in. There are companies that will create this for you; it's not something you want to try at home. Typically, a DCP will cost between $1,000 and $3,000, depending on the specs you require (4K, 3-D, a type of encryption). This will be part of your delivery-items list and you may need more than one.

Delivering your film has hundreds of moving parts and pieces, especially if you are delivering to a distributor for theatrical or to a major platform such as Netflix or Amazon. In addition to the parts of your film, you'll need advertising materials, thumbnails of your posters, a long description, a short description, trailers—all of this is usually referred to as your metadata. If you look at Netflix, you'll see all the information about any film. That is all required in order to complete delivery, and everything will have to go through a QC process, usually performed by a third-party aggregator assigned by the platform.

Each one of these steps is key to whether or not your film will be received as something professionally created or slapped together by a hack. It can be daunting, for sure. I have to admit, even as I write this, I accept that this is an area in which I especially require support. Definitely ask for help if you're not sure.

MARKETING AND DISTRIBUTION

SECTION VI

CONGRATULATIONS: YOU'VE FINISHED YOUR FILM! NOW WHAT?! In your business plan, you outlined the audience for your film and what your possible distribution outlets might be. Now is the time to see if that was true. What was the current state of distribution a year ago may not be true now. How do you figure out what the best possible distribution scenario is for your film?

For many, we don't know what we have until we're done. I often wait until I'm finished with a film to determine exactly what I am going to do with it, even if I've been exploring film festivals and distribution options. What happens when you've entered all those festivals and didn't get into the ones you wanted? What do you do if the film you set out to make is better as a short or a web series? Now is the time to really look at the best avenue to reach your audience and pay back your investors.

It seems that just about every week there is a new digital platform available for you to sell your film. Do you think you have an Oscars contender? Are you creating a strategic partnership with a big brand or organization? In the coming chapters, I will outline each one of these scenarios and how to best approach them. The reality is that it is a buyer's market when it comes to content, so having multiple options at the ready will help you choose the right path for your film.

CHAPTER 16

Film Festivals

For most filmmakers, film festivals provide the best opportunity to get a distribution deal. Many distributors make it their business to be at the big ones and even some of the smaller, more niche film festivals.

The reality is that film festivals are big business, and almost every city has at least one and some more than one. There are film festivals for LGBTQ subjects, women in film, minorities in film, horror, documentary, and so on.

Some people use the "enter all of them" approach and see what happens. If you want to have a ton of laurels (those nifty leaves you can add to your poster that say something like "Official Selection" or "Winner, Best Documentary"), go for it . . . but I'm not sure if this actually helps anything. Some say that it shows distributors there is an audience for your film, especially if you're being chosen for—and/or winning at—some of the bigger festivals, like Sundance, Toronto, Berlin, or even some of the smaller yet still prestigious ones, such as Telluride, Palm Springs, DOC NYC. Yes, this will definitely help.

If you're only being accepted into smaller local festivals, then it's probably not worth it to enter all of them.

I suggest entering the big ones no matter what, as long as it's in your schedule. Sundance entries are early fall, Tribeca is late fall, and Toronto usually opens in February. Try to time your postproduction process to have the ability to enter at least two to three of the major festivals, even ones abroad. If you can, make sure your film is in at least one of the film markets as well, like AFM (in the fall) or Cannes (in May) since buyers are sure to be at those events.

If you're going to enter into smaller ones, look for festivals that might fit your niche. Are you an all-female crew? Does your film focus on a social issue or a minority group? If there is a film festival in your hometown, the hometown of a key member of your team, or the hometown where your film takes place, enter those. You are more likely to get media attention if you're local. All media and images from your event are good PR to share with your followers and include in your press kits for future festivals.

One of my favorite film festivals is SIFF, aka the Seattle International Film Festival. I suggest looking at film festivals in other major cities. Will your film play better in the Midwest or on the East Coast? This helps show distributors that people want to see your film, and a good showing at a major-market film festival could open the door to a theatrical showing in that market. If you can get the butts into the seats at a festival, if you garner glowing reviews, or especially if you win, it's a good indicator for distributors. Again, this is most effective with established film festivals and less likely with the smaller ones.

Film festivals around Los Angeles or New York, even if they are on the smaller side, are usually a good bet as well. Buyers may go simply because it's close to where they live, they are looking for something unique, and they have already heard about or seen everything in the major film festivals. Long Beach has a well-attended festival, so does Palm Springs, and there are tons of local film festivals in Los Angeles and New York that get a good attendance. These festivals also offer the best opportunity for networking, which is one of the main reasons to go to a festival.

Film festivals cost money to enter, and many have different requirements. Some will allow rough cuts, and some will allow you to have already been in distribution (some only digital and some theatrical as well). You will need to check with each festival and be clear about their guidelines before you enter. Some will require you to commit to a world premiere or a territorial premiere (by country). It's sort of a waiting game because you don't want to commit your world premiere to a smaller festival and then get accepted into a bigger one. Most festival organizers are savvy about this. If you get accepted by a smaller festival, take it. If you get accepted by Sundance after that, well, try not to burn any bridges.

Film festivals also cost money to travel to and to promote properly. Some festivals will offer a stipend or accommodations for you to show up, but most won't.

If you intend to use film festivals as a part of your marketing strategy, then budget for it beforehand. Make sure to include entry fees as well as travel and marketing expenses for the actual festival. The reasons to go to a festival are to network, get your film seen by potential distributors and buyers, and begin to build an audience. If you go, make it worth your while.

If you get into a bigger festival like Sundance, hire a publicist. You've made it that far, so it's worth every penny to have a publicist working for you to get media and exposure. If distributors see there is a buzz about your film, they are more likely to check it out.

With Sundance, as with most festivals, it's about being there and getting people to choose your movie as one they want to see. Have postcards with your screening information at the ready and hand them out to people you meet. Put them in local places close to the venue, and don't count on the film-festival organizers to get people to your film. Market yourself and your film—that's why you're there.

If you make it into a big festival and you've never sold a film before, you may want to hire a producer's representative or a sales agent in addition to a publicist. This is a person who has relationships with distributors who can help you with the sale of your film. (FYI: you can hire one even if you aren't going to festivals.)

A sales agent is usually tied to a firm that represents your film to domestic and foreign buyers and attends film markets such as AFM or Cannes, and a producer's representative is usually an independent. Not always true, but mostly true.

A word of caution about producer's reps: get references and do your homework on them. There are a lot of people who claim they are reps but they haven't sold a thing. There isn't any regulatory body for people who call themselves producer's reps, so it's up to you not to get scammed. A good representative will have no issue giving you references. A producer's rep's job is to secure you a deal, connect you with potential buyers at festivals (or before or after), and assist you in the negotiation.

Some will require a fee up front and many will want an executive producer credit. Make this contingent on them securing and negotiating the deal.

Here is an example of a producer's representation agreement wherein they receive a commission based on adjusted gross receipts and an executive producer screen credit. As with all the contracts I include in this book, consult with an attorney prior to using.

WHEREAS {Sales Representative Name} ("Representation") has entered into an agreement acting as Representation & Executive Producer for the production entitled {PRODUCTION} (the "Program"); and

WHEREAS {Artist's Name} ("Artist") is the producer of, and owns all right, title and interest, including copyright, in and to, a production entitled {PRODUCTION}; and

WHEREAS {Artist's Name} ("Artist") wishes to retain the services of {Sales Representative Name} ("Representation") to act as Representation & Executive Producer of the Program;

NOW THEREFORE THIS AGREEMENT WITNESSES that in consideration of the premises, mutual covenants and agreements herein and other good and valuable consideration, the sufficiency of which is hereby acknowledged, the parties agree as follows:

1. Grant of Representation Rights
(a) The Artist grants to Representation the exclusive right, license, and privilege to act as Representation & Executive Producer of the Program and any derivatives in all languages and versions and digital formats in all media now known or in future devised, including all upgrades, enhancements, modifications and functional substitutions therefore, throughout the Territory

for the applicable Term, including but not limited to the right to license the Program or components thereof to broadcasters or other licensees.

2. Term and Territory

(a) The Term of this Agreement shall continue in perpetuity on the execution of this Agreement unless terminated in accordance with this Agreement.

(b) The Territory of this Agreement shall be the world, universe, and any unknown universes that may become known.

3. Representation

(a) Representation agrees to use commercially reasonable efforts consistent with industry standards to accurately represent the Program as Representation & Executive Producer.

4. Producer's Content

(a) Artist shall own and retain all right, title, and interest, including but not limited to copyright, in and to all original creative elements developed and produced by the Artist for the Program from the inception of the creation thereof and in perpetuity.

5. (Sales Representative Name) Contacts, Technology, and Content

(a) Representation shall own all right, title, and interest, including but not limited to copyright, in and to all original and pre-existing source code, site files, applications, tools, methods, programs, software and know-how created or used by Representation in the promotion and sales of the Program and all original creative elements developed and produced from the inception of the creation thereof and in perpetuity and have the right to exploit independently from the Program with no payments being due or payable to Artist from such exploitation. Representation makes no warranty of any kind that the contacts, technologies, or content will always be available, accessible, uninterrupted, timely, secure, or operate without error.

6. Representation Commission

(a) Representation shall be entitled to retain ____% of Gross Receipts or Adjusted Receipts, as applicable, as its commission earned for the total sales made by the program.

7. Executive Producer Commission

(a) Representation shall be paid ____% of Gross Receipts or Adjusted Receipts of the total sales made by the Program, as applicable, as payment earned for Executive Producing.

8. Inspection of Books and Records

(a) The Artist shall maintain in the state of California proper books and records in relation to the matters set out in this Agreement and in accordance with generally accepted accounting principles. For the purposes of verifying the accuracy of the Reports and the remittance of Net Receipts, Representation or its authorized agent shall be entitled, during normal business hours and upon 48 hours prior notice, to examine at its own expense such books and records, and may at any time and at its own expense require an audit of such books and records.

9. Producer's Representations and Warranties

(a) The Artist represents and warrants to Representation:

(i) That it owns all right title and interest, or has acquired all the necessary licenses and grants of rights, including but not limited to copyright, in and to the Program and has the right to enter into this Agreement and to grant to Representation the distribution rights herein granted;

(ii) That no part of the Program or the exercise by Representation of the rights herein granted will violate or infringe upon any rights of any third party, including but not limited to copyright, trademark rights, or any other proprietary right or interest of any kind; and

(iii) That the Program does not contain any defamatory or illegal material or violate any law.

10. Executive Producer Credit

(a) The form of the Executive Producer's credit on any screen, computer screen, paid advertising, phonograph records, books, tapes, videodiscs, videocassettes and the containers thereof, when and as required, shall be "Executive Produced by {Sales Representative Name}." The words "Executive Produced by" on-screen shall be at least one-half the size of type used to accord title credit of the program/production. The Artist involved shall be bound by such determination, and if notified thereof by the Executive Producer in writing within a reasonable time before prints with the main titles are prepared but shall not be bound with respect to advertising, publicity, or other material prepared prior to such notice.

11. Restriction on Use of Words "Executive Producer"

(a) The Artist will not hereafter and during the term hereof enter into any agreement with any guild, craft, union, or labor organization in which it agrees to accord members thereof credit on-screen, paid advertising, phonograph records, books, tapes (including the cover of the book, record, or tape as well as any album, envelope, box, or other container in which such record or tape is contained) which includes the words "Executive Producer," or any derivation thereof, but the foregoing shall not apply to a guild or craft with which the Artist heretofore entered into an agreement requiring credit.

(b) Except as required by agreements heretofore executed by the Artist, and agreements permitted by subparagraph above to be hereafter executed, Artist will not grant to any individual, other than Representation, any credit which includes the words "Executive Producer," or any derivation thereof.

12. Screen Credit

Representation will receive credit of the Program and shall be accorded credit on all positive prints and all videodiscs/videocassettes of the film in size of type not less than fifty percent (50%) of the size in which the title of the production is displayed or of the largest size in which credit is accorded to any other person, whichever is greater. No other credit shall appear on the card which accords credit to the Executive Producer of the Program. Such credit shall be on the last title card appearing prior to principal photography. After such copies are furnished, there can be no changes relating to the term Executive Producer or any derivation thereof.

13. Visibility of Executive Producer's Name

Artist pledges to use its best efforts to improve the visibility of the Executive Producer's name in publicity.

14. Publicity

In any formal publicity released by the Artist, whenever the name of the picture is mentioned, the name of the Executive Producer shall also be mentioned.

15. Alternative Medium Credit

The following paragraph is applicable to any medium which the Artist distributes or licenses for distribution. The Executive Producer shall be given credit on all medium articles identified with the production hereunder or the container thereof, if credit is accorded to any other person who rendered services or performed in connection with the production.

16. Distribution and Licensing Agreements

Artist shall provide in any contract with any and all distributors that the distributor shall be bound for the benefit of the Employees and the director to all of the provisions of the Directors Guild of America's basic agreement and the individual employment agreements relating to credit. The Producer shall not be held responsible to Executive Producer for breach of contract by the distributor.

17. Assumption of Obligations

Artist shall specifically contract with its distributors and the television networks that they shall not cut, edit, move, or omit the credit of the Director as placed by the Employer on the positive prints.

18. Indemnification

(a) Artist shall indemnify and save harmless Representation, its assigns and licensees from and against any and all losses, damages, actions or causes of action, suits, claims, demands, penalties, and interest arising in connection with or out of the Producer's breach of any representation and warranty.

19. Notice

(a) Any notice required or permitted to be given hereunder shall be in writing and shall be deemed given (i) when delivered personally to any officer of the party being notified; or (ii) on the third business day after being sent by registered or certified mail, postage prepaid, facsimile telecopier, to predetermined addresses.

20. Force Majeure

(a) Neither party hereto shall be responsible for any losses or damages to the other occasioned by delays in the performance or non-performance of any of said party's obligations when caused by acts of God, strike, acts of war, inability of supplies or material or labor, or any other cause beyond the reasonable control of the said party.

21. Severability

(a) In the event any portion of this Agreement is deemed to be invalid or unenforceable, such portion shall be deemed severed and the parties agree that the remaining portions of this Agreement shall remain in full force and effect.

22. Assignment

(a) Neither party may assign or otherwise transfer this Agreement without the written consent of the other party. This Agreement shall ensure to the benefit of and bind the parties hereto and their respective legal representatives, successors, and assigns.

23. Confidentiality

(a) All logistical and financial terms with respect to this Agreement shall be treated by the Parties as strictly confidential other than as may be disclosed by either Party to accountants and lawyers giving advice to the Parties, or in the course of enforcement of any provision hereof.

24. Governing Law

(a) This Agreement shall be governed by and construed in accordance with the laws of the state of {insert state} in the country of the United States. As either parties option, any controversy or claim arising out of or relating to this contract or the breach thereof (except for an action for injunctive relief) may be resolved by arbitration held in {insert county} County, State of {insert state}, in accordance with the Rules of the American Arbitration Association in effect at the time the arbitration is initiated, and judgment upon the award rendered by the arbitrators may be entered in any court jurisdiction thereof.

25. Entire Agreement

(a) This Agreement, including the recitals and Schedules, sets forth the entire agreement between the parties with respect to the subject matter hereof and the Agreement shall be amended only by a writing signed by the parties.

26. Counterparts

(a) This Agreement may be executed in counterparts in the same form and such parts so executed shall together form one original document and be read and construed as if one copy of the Agreement had been executed.

IN WITNESS WHEREOF the parties hereto have executed this Agreement effective this ____ of, _____, 20____.

Per: _____
Authorized Signatory: {Representation Name}

Per: _____
Authorized Signatory: {This is where your name goes.}

How do you find producers' reps? That is a great question. Most of them aren't listed in some nifty phone book. AFM usually has a list, or you could look at IMDbPro.

As a side note: it's good to list your film on IMDb as soon as you are serious about getting it made. You can update it as you move along, adding crew, trailers, etc. Anyone who is considering your film will most likely start there. I'm not a fan of the IMDb interface for uploading your information, but it's something you should do early. Joining IMDbPro is also helpful because you can find additional information about other films, such as who their distributor, sales agent, or even producer's representative was and start by contacting them. You can also find box office information and other information about the film not available on IMDb.

Networking is key when it comes to selling your film. Go where they hang out, which is film markets, conferences, and, of course, festivals.

At any festival, show up to work it. Have business cards, your website ready, a way to collect e-mail addresses and information easily. If you can reach out to the local press who will be covering the event and share a press kit of your film, you want to try and generate a buzz about your film.

What's in a press kit? A press kit can be digital—you could create a webpage—but it's also good to have some printouts that you can leave with media contacts. It should include links to the film's website, trailer, and social media pages, as well as bios of the key players (e.g., producer, director, main characters), especially anyone who is noteworthy. If you can have any of your subjects attend the festival with you (especially if they can generate interest from the media), you should. They are also a great draw for an audience showing up to your film and staying for the Q and A session after your screening(s). If you're going to go to a festival, go for as much as possible. If you've bought the plane ticket and paid for the hotel, you should use the opportunity to network. Show up to all the events and talk to other filmmakers.

Use this as an opportunity to generate buzz on social media. Your followers want to see you at the events.

A brief note about using social media: if you haven't already created your social platforms for the film, you should begin right when you enter film festivals. I highly suggest starting them as early as possible to begin to build interest in your film. If you have a robust social media presence, it will help you get a distribution deal. I will discuss ways to use social media in Chapter 19.

Film festivals don't typically look at your social media following as criteria for accepting you; they should be choosing based solely on the content/quality of your film. But hey, you never know who's looking at what, so why not have as much going for you as possible?

CHAPTER 17

Theatrical and Third-Party Distributors

Everybody wants their film to be in theaters. It's a huge ego boost to stand in the back of a full theater and see your name and your film on the big screen. Some films are destined for the big screen, and some will be better received via a digital platform such as Netflix, or you may better serve your film to release on a smaller, more niche platform or direct to YouTube. It's also possible to do a combination of all of the above.

Let's get the big question out of the way. If you want to go for an Academy Award, you *must* release your film for at least seven days in *both* Los Angeles and New York in a legitimate theater. Laemmle, ArcLight, and Landmark count, as do the major theaters, but they may be harder to land. There are other requirements in addition to the cities and number of days. Be sure and confirm them on the Academy of Motion Picture Arts and Science's website since they sometimes change.

There are companies that offer something called an "Oscar Qualifying Package," which, for a fee, will help you secure the requirements for academy consideration. The fee depends on how many theaters you want to open in, and the entire cost is somewhere around $30,000. This includes the theater rental, ads and other marketing, and a PR person, etc. It's actually a good deal since it's likely you'll spend that much going it alone. CINEMAflix Distribution is one company offering this service. They also offer DVD sales and VOD placement.

If you want to go it alone, you can contact the main office of one of the smaller theaters and simply rent the theater, or explain you're going for an academy consideration and offer them a ticket-sales guarantee. If your film does well, they may even hold it for a second week. You will need to make sure to follow the academy's advertising and other guidelines and either get your own press and reviews or hire a PR person. Even if you're not interested in becoming academy-eligible, you can still book the film in any theater yourself by using this method.

Netflix, HBO, and other major cable outlets will do a theatrical release if they feel the film warrants it. The big question is how do you get your film to them?

You can either know someone who knows someone or generate enough buzz about your film that they take an interest. This is where attending film festivals, holding screenings of the film on your own, getting media attention, and building your social platform help.

If, after your festival run, you still don't have a deal and you still believe your film has what it takes to generate buzz, go ahead and set up some limited theatrical screenings yourself, if you can fund it properly. You don't have to open in Los Angeles or New York first. I have, on many occasions, opened a film in a market where I knew there was a strong audience for the film, put money into the marketing there, and then through the success of that run, added others. I'll explain how to do this in the next chapter.

If your goal is to get a distribution deal and let them figure it out, then focus on getting your film seen by the buyers. This is at film markets, through an agent or producer's rep or personal relationships. If all that fails, you can work with an aggregator.

An aggregator is a company that funnels films into multiple digital platforms. This is a pay-to-play service where you pay a fee depending on the number of platforms you want your film to appear on. You deliver to them, and they run the QC and submit your film for you. You are not always guaranteed to land on Netflix or Hulu, but you will get on places like Comcast, Time Warner, etc. For most of these services, they charge a fee up front and then you get to keep the revenues.

You can attempt to go it alone platform by platform, but I don't recommend it.

Don't discount platforms and cable networks such as the Sundance Channel, IFC, A&E, History Channel, Travel Channel, ESPN Sports, or even CNN or other major news networks. These channels have started to spend big bucks in the last few years for original content, especially documentaries.

Below is a sample Distributors Agreement, and as I have said, always have any agreement reviewed by your legal counsel.

Sample All-Rights Distribution Agreement between Producer and Distributor

---

XXX DISTRIBUTOR DISTRIBUTION RIGHTS AGREEMENT

This Distribution Rights Agreement (the "Agreement") is effective as of _____ of _____, 20____ (the "Effective Date"), by and between XXX ("Distributor"), and YYY Productions ("Licensor"), with regard to the motion picture entitled "ABC" (the "Picture").

1. GRANTED RIGHTS:

(a) Licensor hereby exclusively and irrevocably (subject to the terms and conditions herein) grants to Distributor throughout the License Period (as defined below) and the Licensed Territory (as defined below) all distribution and exploitation rights of every kind in and relating to the Picture including, without limitation, the sole and exclusive right, license and privilege under copyright to, and to authorize, license and sublicense others to exhibit, distribute, transmit, reproduce, manufacture, publicly display, project, publicly perform, advertise, promote, and otherwise exploit the Picture (including clip and footage licenses related to the Picture) in any and all media or medium, now or hereafter devised, by all means of transmission and delivery, now known or hereafter devised, in all languages, and in all versions, including, without limitation, all forms of theatrical and nontheatrical exhibition, ancillary exhibition (e.g., airlines, ships, and military bases), all forms of home video (including but not limited to electronic sell through and rental, videocassettes, DVDs, and CD-ROMs), all forms of television exhibition (including but not limited to free television, basic and pay cable, pay per view, and all forms of on-demand), and all means of digital exhibition including without limitation to broadband, mobile, internet streaming, and online transmission and delivery (collectively, the "Granted Rights"). The parties agree that the Granted Rights shall include the right to advertise and promote the Picture in the Licensed Territory (and if the Licensed Territory hereunder is not worldwide, then nonexclusively worldwide with respect to advertising and promoting on the internet, provided that any such internet or online promotion, or promotion by similar technologies/mediums which are accessible outside the Licensed Territory, shall limit the display of clips and trailers of the Picture to no more than three {3} minutes in length) in any manner or media, now known or hereafter devised, including, without limitation, the right to use and license others to use Licensor's name and the title of trailers created for and excerpts from the Picture (including audio portions only) and the name, voice, and likeness of and any biographical material furnished by Licensor concerning all main cast and key crew (including the producers of the Picture) appearing in or connected with the Picture for the purpose of advertising, promoting, and/or publicizing the Picture, the Distributor, the licensee, and/or the program service on which the Picture is exhibited, subject to any reasonable and customary third-party contractual restrictions of which Licensor has notified Distributor in writing as part of Delivery (as defined in Paragraph 9(b) below). As between Licensor and Distributor, all rights of exploitation of the Picture which do not involve the distribution or exhibition of the Picture or excerpts thereof (the "Reserved Rights"), including, without limitation, sound track album, music publishing, novelization, or other publication rights are hereby reserved to Licensor.

Distributor acknowledges that Licensor has employed a third-party television sales agent for the purposes of television sales in the United States. Until the date that is three (3) months from the Effective Date of this Agreement (the "Television Sales Holdback"), Distributor shall not solicit television sales. Licensor agrees that it shall terminate effective the end of Television Sales Holdback any and all third-party television sales representation and that Distributor shall have the sole right to solicit and execute any television sales agreements.

(b) All sequel, prequel, remake, and television production rights (e.g., episodic series, miniseries, and movies of the week) in connection with the Picture (each, a "Subsequent Production Right") shall be retained by Licensor but shall be deemed "frozen" (i.e., may not be licensed or exploited) until three (3) years after the US Home Video release date.

(c) To effectuate the Granted Rights, Licensor shall execute concurrently herewith, the Instruction of Transfer attached as Exhibit A.

2. LICENSED TERRITORY: Worldwide (the "Licensed Territory").

3. LICENSE PERIOD: Commencing as of the Effective Date and continuing for seven (7) years from the Delivery (as defined in clause 9(b) the "License Period").

4. PARTICIPATION IN NET RECEIPTS:
(a) Distributor agrees to pay to Licensor one hundred percent (100%) of Net Receipts. "Net Receipts" shall mean Gross Receipts after deduction for (i) payment to Distributor of the Distribution Fee as defined below in clauses 4.(a) 1–4; (iii) all

costs and expenses incurred by Distributor in connection with the promotion, distribution, and exploitation of the Picture, in any manner and media, including, without limitation, all manufacturing and packaging costs for HV Devices (as defined herein) (the "Distribution Expenses"). If the Picture is licensed for distribution as part of a package or library including other programming (e.g., via subscription video on-demand), Distributor shall evaluate the Picture individually and allocate a share of gross receipts derived therefrom and the related expenses to the Picture as Distributor determines in its good faith judgment based on the fair market value or usage of the Picture, as the case may be.

The "Distribution Fee" shall be an amount equal to:

1. 35% of theatrical revenues;
2. 35% with respect to all digital rights;
3. 50% with respect to all ancillary rights;

with respect to all forms of theatrical and nontheatrical rights; with respect to all forms of television rights; with respect to all forms of home video rights;

(b) amounts actually received by or credited to Distributor from the exercise of the Granted Rights after deduction for all refunds, credits, discounts, allowances, rebates, and set-offs, and a provision for reserves against returns and credits (which such reserves shall not exceed twenty-five percent (25%) of Home Video Device gross receipts, which shall be liquidated not less frequently than every twelve {12} months).

5. PAYMENT; ACCOUNTING:

(a) Commencing with the first calendar quarter in which gross receipts in respect of the Picture are received by Distributor and on a quarterly basis for two years and, thereafter, on a semi-annual basis, Distributor shall furnish Licensor with a reasonably detailed statement showing the gross receipts, distribution expenses, calculation of Net Receipts, and the amount, if any, due to Licensor with respect to such period. Each statement shall be delivered to Licensor at the address listed in the first paragraph of this Agreement within sixty (60) days after the end of any applicable period in which Gross Receipts are received and shall be accompanied by payment of any amounts due to Licensor in US dollars, subject to all laws and regulations requiring the deduction or withholding of payments for income or other taxes payable by or assessable against Licensor. All statements shall be deemed true and accurate and conclusively binding upon Licensor if not disputed by Licensor in writing within eighteen (18) months after the delivery of such statement and if a formal legal action is not commenced by Licensor within one year after such written objection. For the avoidance of doubt, if a formal legal action is commenced by Licensor, all statements to which such claim pertains shall not be deemed binding upon Licensor until such claim is resolved.

(b) Licensor shall have the right, at its own expense {subject to the last sentence of this clause (b)}, on at least thirty (30) days prior written notice to Distributor, to have a certified public accountant examine the books of account with regard to the exploitation of the Picture at Distributor's principal place of business during normal business hours, but not more than once annually and for not more than one consecutive thirty- (30-) day period during each annual period (provided that the books and records are timely made available to such auditor). Such right of examination shall be limited solely to inspection of books and records pertaining to the Picture (and no information related to allocations of revenues or expenses shall be redacted from such books and records) for the period three years prior to the date of the most recent statement provided by Distributor.

6. DISTRIBUTION AND MARKETING: Distributor shall have complete discretion and control as to the time, manner, and terms of distribution, exhibition, licensing, exploitation, advertising, and marketing of the Picture (including the unrestricted right to use sublicensees or subdistributors, except for the initial theatrical distribution of the Picture), including without limitation any decision to make the Picture available for video-on-demand exhibition day and date with the theatrical release of the Picture; provided, however, that Distributor shall consult with Licensor with respect to the marketing strategy for the initial theatrical release of the Picture, it being understood and agreed that Distributor's decisions shall be controlling with respect to all such matters. Distributor makes no guarantees, warranties, or representations as to the amount of Net Receipts that may be derived from the Picture.

7. CREDITS:

(a) Distributor shall have the right, at its expense, to include its (or any of its affiliates, subdistributors, or licensees) names, logos, trademarks and/or emblems, in such manner, position, and form as Distributor may elect and is customary in the motion picture industry (including a presentation credit), on all prints and copies of the Picture and on all advertising and publicity materials for the Picture, together with all appropriate text, as determined by Distributor in its sole discretion, indicating that the Picture is being distributed by Distributor.

(b) Distributor shall adhere to Licensor's contractual credit and paid advertising obligations to third parties and shall notify the licensees of Distributor with regard to such obligations, provided that Distributor receives timely written notice of such obligations and that such obligations are reasonable and customary in the motion picture industry. The casual or inadvertent failure by Distributor or the failure of any third party to comply with such obligations shall not be a breach hereof. Within a reasonable period following receipt of written notice from Licensor specifying the details of any failure by Distributor or any licensee of Distributor to comply with contractual credit or paid advertising obligations, Distributor will notify any applicable licensee regarding such failure and will take such steps as are reasonably and economically practicable to cure such failure prospectively with respect to copies of the Picture not yet made and advertisements for the Picture issued by or under the control of Distributor which have not yet been placed.

8. COPYRIGHT: The copyright in the Picture will be held by Licensor, and Licensor shall register, renew, extend, and protect such copyright in Licensor's name for the maximum period of time allowed by law and furnish Distributor with copies of such registrations. If Licensor fails to do so, Distributor shall have the right to register the copyright in Producer's name in the U.S. Copyright Office, the cost of which shall be a Distribution Expense. In addition, Distributor shall have the right, subject to prior consultation with Licensor, to take such steps and to institute such suits and proceedings as Distributor may deem necessary or advisable to protect the copyright in the Picture and its elements and to prevent any infringement of the Granted Rights, all of which costs shall be deemed Distribution Expenses, provided that any and all recoveries shall be included in the gross receipts for purposes of calculating Net Receipts. Licensor shall have the right to participate in any such legal proceedings with counsel of its choice at its expense. In connection with the foregoing, Licensor hereby irrevocably appoints Distributor as its attorney-in-fact with the full power to execute any and all documents as may reasonably be required consistent with the terms of this Agreement. This appointment shall be a power coupled with an interest. Distributor shall provide copies to Licensor of any material documents executed by Distributor pursuant to such power of attorney.

9. DELIVERY:

(a) The Picture shall: (i) be an original sound motion picture, photographed in color using 35mm, with an aspect ratio of 2.35:1, in the English language; (ii) have a running time (including main and end titles) of approximately one hundred (100) minutes in length; (iii) be the version that was screened for _____ and (iv) be directed by _____, written by _____, produced by _____, and starring _____.

(b) Licensor agrees that time is of the essence with respect to Delivery and that Delivery shall occur no later than ___ of _____, 20___ (the "Delivery Date"). The "Delivery" of the Picture shall mean (i) delivery of, at Distributor's cost and expense (subject to the following sentence), or access to the Picture and all items listed on the Delivery Schedule attached hereto as Exhibit B (the "Delivery Schedule") of a technical quality acceptable to Distributor (such acceptance not to be unreasonably withheld or delayed) that Distributor has ordered from Licensor (the "Delivery Materials") to the address specified by Distributor or to an appropriate laboratory (provided that Distributor has received an executed laboratory access letter in the form attached to the Delivery Schedule). Prior to the delivery or creation of any Delivery Materials in connection with the Delivery of the Picture, Licensor shall provide the applicable price list to Distributor and Distributor shall preapprove all such delivery costs and expenses to be paid by Distributor prior to Licensor effecting Delivery hereunder, which costs and expenses shall be recouped by Distributor as Distribution Expenses. If Distributor notifies Licensor of any Delivery deficiencies, then Licensor shall have ten (10) business days within which to cure all such delivery deficiencies. If Licensor fails to timely deliver the Picture or to cure any delivery deficiencies within the aforesaid cure period, then Distributor may at its election (A) secure acceptable replacements for the deficient Delivery Materials and charge such costs as Distribution Expenses or (B) terminate this Agreement upon written notice to Licensor, in which event any Advance paid to Licensor prior thereto shall be repaid to Distributor in full. Unless Distributor elects to terminate this Agreement, under no circumstance shall Licensor be relieved of its obligation to make complete Delivery nor shall Distributor be deemed to have waived any Delivery requirements. Acceptance by Distributor of less than all of the Delivery Materials and/or release of the Picture by Distributor prior to delivery of all of the Delivery Materials shall not be deemed to relieve Licensor of its obligations to Distributor pursuant to the warranties and indemnification provisions of this Agreement.

(c) Upon the expiration of the License Period, in accordance with Licensor's written instructions and at Licensor's sole cost and expense, Distributor shall deliver or destroy the Delivery Materials provided by Licensor hereunder and any materials created in connection with the Picture by Distributor (other than customary archival materials for the internal use of Distributor).

10. EDITING AND MODIFICATIONS: Distributor shall have the right to cut, edit, delete from, dub and subtitle the Picture as Distributor in its sole discretion shall determine is necessary: (a) to subtitle or dub the Picture as is customary for exploitation of the Picture; (b) to avoid legal liability; (c) to conform the Picture to meet the requirements of a governmental censorship authority or comply with local or national broadcast standards or any other applicable laws or standards (including obscenity laws or standards); (d) to create closed caption versions; (e) to insert bugs, advertising, sponsorships, or other commercial materials (including, without limitation, such promotional and commercial material that may run concurrently with the end credits); (f) to squeeze and compress the film and the credits in a manner which is then current in the motion picture and television industries; (g) to create promotional materials; and (h) to create and license clips from the Picture in a manner which is customary in the motion picture and television industries, and/or to authorize any person to do the foregoing. With respect to any editing of the Picture for the purposes set forth in clauses (b) or (c), or in any manner other than as described in this Paragraph, such editing shall be subject to the written approval of Licensor, provided that if Licensor has failed to respond to Distributor within 5 business days after receipt of Distributor's notice of requested editing or if Licensor accepts such offer but is not ready and willing to do so when reasonably required by Distributor, such editing shall be deemed approved and Distributor shall have the right to make such edits or to cause a third party to make such edits.

11. DEFERRED FEES; RESIDUALS: The calculation and payment of any and all residuals, deferred fees, and/or third party participations shall be the responsibility of Licensor alone. The Picture is not under the jurisdiction of any guild and Distributor shall have no guild residual obligations.

12. SECURITY INTEREST: As security for the rights and entitlements of Distributor hereunder, Licensor hereby grants and assigns to Distributor a mortgage of copyright and a continuing security interest in all of Licensor's right, title, and interest in and to the Granted Rights hereunder and all proceeds thereof. Licensor agrees to execute all such documents as Distributor may reasonably require in order to effectuate the security interest, including the Mortgage of Copyright and Power of Attorney attached hereto as Exhibit C.

13. LICENSOR DEFAULT: At Distributor's option and upon written notice given to Licensor, Distributor shall have the right to terminate this Agreement and shall be entitled to immediate repayment of all out-of-pocket costs incurred by Distributor in connection with the Picture and may declare all obligations hereunder due and owing and may proceed to enforce payment and performance by Licensor and exercise all of Distributor's rights and remedies at law or equity, if (i) Licensor breaches any material covenant, agreement, or obligation under this Agreement and fails to cure such breach within forty-eight (48) hours after receipt of written notice from Distributor {except such right to cure shall not apply to Licensor's failure to timely deliver the Picture by the Delivery Date in accordance with Paragraph 9(b)}; (ii) any representation or warranty made by Licensor is untrue or incomplete in any material respect on or as of the date made; or (iii) Licensor becomes insolvent or a petition under any bankruptcy or insolvency law shall be filed by or against Licensor or any property of Licensor is attached and such attachment is not released within 30 days or if Licensor executes an assignment for the benefit of creditors or if a receiver, custodian, liquidator, or trustee is appointed for Licensor. Without limiting any other remedies available to it hereunder or by law, Distributor shall have the right to withhold and reserve from any monies whatsoever payable to Licensor hereunder, sums reasonably sufficient to secure Distributor from and against Licensor's liabilities or the material breach of any of its obligations under this Agreement.

14. REPRESENTATIONS, WARRANTIES, AND INDEMNITIES: Licensor hereby represents and warrants that (i) it has the full right, power, and authority to enter into this Agreement and to grant the rights granted herein, (ii) Licensor owns or controls all rights in and to the Picture and in and to all literary, dramatic, and musical material included therein required for Distributor to exercise the Granted Rights, without any lien, claim, or other encumbrance thereon, (iii) all musical compositions and/or performances of musical compositions contained in the Picture have been licensed for in-context use, out-of-context use (including use in advertising and publicity of the Picture and the DVD menu) in all media, now known, worldwide, for the duration of the License Period, and no additional payment for the use of any such composition or performance shall be required except for payment of the applicable performance rights fees to ASCAP, BMI, or SESAC, if applicable, and payment of new use or reuse fees in connection with master recordings, if applicable, (iv) all licenses of any material licensed for use in connection with the Picture contain language to the substantive effect that the licensor of such material has not and shall not commit any act likely to prevent or hinder the full enjoyment of the rights that are licensed hereunder, (v) no part of the Picture nor the exhibition, distribution, exploitation, promotion, or other use of the Picture by Distributor or its licensees will violate or infringe upon any rights of any third party, (vi) there are no guilds or unions that may claim jurisdiction over the services to be rendered hereunder and no collective bargaining agreements covering the Picture, and (vii) there is no action, suit, claim, or proceeding pending, affecting, or threatened against the Picture, its producers, Licensor, or any distributor of the Picture. Licensor shall indemnify, defend (at Distributor's election), and hold harmless Distributor and its officers, agents, employees, affiliates, and licensees and assigns from and against any and all claims, damages, liabilities, costs and expenses, including reasonable outside attorneys' fees and disbursements, arising out of (A) any breach or, in connection with a third-party claim, alleged breach of any representation, warranty, covenant, or agreement made by Licensor herein, (B) the exercise by Distributor of the Granted Rights in accordance with this Agreement, or (C) the violation or infringement of the rights of any third party as a result of the exhibition, distribution, exploitation, promotion, or other use of the Picture by Distributor or its licensees in accordance with this Agreement.

15. INSURANCE: Licensor shall (at its own cost and expense) provide and maintain, in full force and effect for a period of three years from Delivery, a liability insurance (errors and omissions coverage) policy or policies that covers any and all claims arising out of or relating to errors and omissions related to media liability for the Picture and the title thereof with a deductible of no more than $10,000 and with minimum limits of at least $1,000,000 for any claim arising out of single occurrence and $3,000,000 in the aggregate for the Picture. Licensor shall name Distributor, its parent, affiliates, subsidiaries, assigns, and licensees as now or hereafter may exist as additional insureds on such policy.

16. MISCELLANEOUS:

(a) Distributor shall have the right to assign its rights and obligations hereunder to any third party and shall be relieved of its obligations to the extent they are assumed in writing by (i) any purchaser of all or substantially all of its stock or assets, (ii) any entity into which it is merged, consolidated, or combined, (iii) any mini or major studio, or (iv) any affiliate of Distributor. Distributor shall have the right to assign its rights and obligations hereunder to any other third party not listed in clauses (i) through (iv) above, provided that Distributor shall remain primarily liable to Licensor for its obligations hereunder unless prior written approval of such assignment and assumption of Distributor's rights and obligations is obtained from Licensor. Licensor may not assign this Agreement or any of its rights or obligations hereunder, other than its right to receive monies hereunder, without the prior written approval of Distributor (not to be unreasonably withheld).

(b) This agreement shall be governed by and construed in accordance with the laws of the state of {insert state} applicable to contracts made and wholly performed therein without regard to principles of conflicts of law. Each party hereby consents to the jurisdiction of any state or federal court located in the state of {insert state}, city of {insert city}.

(c) Licensor agrees that its rights and remedies in the event of any breach of this Agreement by Distributor will be limited to the right, if any, to recover money damages in an action at law, and in no event will Licensor be entitled by reason of any such breach to seek injunctive or other equitable relief or to enjoin or restrain the distribution, exhibition, advertising, or any other means of exploitation of the Picture or the Granted Rights, except to the extent the Distributor exceeds the scope of the Granted Rights.

(d) This Agreement may not be amended nor any provision waived except in writing signed by the parties hereto. This Agreement contains the full understanding of the parties with respect to the subject matter hereof and supersedes any and all previous agreements between the parties. Each party acknowledges that it is entering into this Agreement in reliance only upon the provisions herein set forth, and not upon any representation, warranty, covenant, agreement, obligation, or other consideration not set forth herein.

(e) All notices from either party to the other in connection herewith shall be given in writing by international courier, messenger, facsimile, or personal delivery, addressed to the parties as first set forth above. The earlier of (i) actual receipt (ii) five days after the date of the receipt from an International courier, and (iii) the date of messengering, faxing (providing there is an electronic "answerback"), or of personal delivery shall be deemed to be the date of service.

(f) This Agreement is comprised of this document as well as Exhibits A, B, and C and Schedules 1 and 2, all of which Exhibits and Schedules are incorporated by this reference.

By signing in the places below, Distributor and Licensor accept and agree to all the terms and conditions of this Agreement as of the date of execution.

YYY PRODUCTIONS
By: _____ Date: _____
{Name, Title}

XXX DISTRIBUTION
By: _____ Date: _____
{Name, Title}

One thing to remember when you work with a distributor: most of them won't put the same effort you will into marketing the film. Ultimately, their effort and funding will depend on how much they believe in the film. Sadly, I have seen many people sign distribution deals thinking they are set, only to find that the distribution company didn't really do much to market the film. They put it into their output-deal pipeline. Many distributors have output deals with Netflix, Comcast, etc., and they need content to provide those platforms. They get money regardless of how the film does, and having a library of films for many distribution companies is a profit center in itself. When negotiating your contract, ask about this and ask them to put in writing their financial and marketing commitment. Are they going to release theatrically? Or does it say they "can" in the contract? (Which means they probably won't.) If they are, how many theaters? Which markets? What is their prints and advertising (aka their P&A, or marketing budget) spend going to be? If you don't want to end up being disappointed after the deal is done, you must find this information out ahead of time.

CHAPTER 18

Self-Distribution and Ancillary Products

Back in 2004, my filmmaking partners and I created what is now used often and called the self-distribution model. Back then, it was almost unheard of for a film to open in theaters without a distributor. Nowadays, almost everyone I know is doing it themselves, especially filmmakers who work on documentaries or niche films.

Earlier I described how you can book a theater yourself. You can either strike a profit-sharing deal with a theater or you can simply rent the theater yourself and keep the revenues. It's sometimes tough to figure who to contact about booking your film in a theater. My advice is to start by contacting the person in charge of renting the theater for private events. It's harder to get booked into a national chain because they usually have regional buyers and they have their screens booked months in advance. Begin with privately owned theaters or art houses (there are still a few around) or smaller chains like iPic, ArcLight, Landmark, etc., and then start with the theater manager.

Typically, a theater keeps 40 percent of the ticket sales, and the rest is split between the distributor and the producer. If you do the math, the theater keeps 40 percent, and the distributor usually takes between 35 and 40 percent, so that leaves you with about 20 percent of the theatrical revenues. Let's not forget that the distributor is going to take off the top any and all expenses related to releasing the film, which means that unless your film is grossing hundreds of thousands of dollars (more like millions), you're likely not going to see any profits from a theatrical release. Remember, to play for one week in Los

Angeles, with all the advertising, delivery elements, etc., it will cost about $15,000 to $20,000. That's for one week, so your film will need to gross triple that in order for you, the producer, to see any profits. In New York, it's more like $25,000 to $30,000 for one week. A theatrical release should really be considered a marketing expense. It's a tool used to generate media and buzz so that you can increase your foreign sales revenue and you can increase your sales figures to pay cable—typically pay cable pays a percentage based on theatrical revenues as the licensing fee for the rights to play your film. These are good reasons to go for a theatrical if you have the budget to properly promote your film and you're confident that you're going to get good reviews and sell enough tickets to show that there is an audience for your film and that it's worth buying.

If you can't get a distributor to do a theatrical release and you want to go it alone, make sure you set yourself up for success. Again, you don't have to start in Los Angeles or New York. You could start in a smaller market, which is probably less expensive, and build a buzz about the film. You can move from theater to theater. Smaller theaters and even some of the mini chains pay attention to what's out there. They are looking for films that can compete with the blockbusters, so choose markets where you have the best chance of selling out and getting held over. A film that can hold for two to three weeks in a market is valuable. Open in your hometown first. Was your film shot in a specific city? Is your film about a specific event or location? Is there a city or market where people work or engage in an activity that relates to your film? Find as big an audience for your film in a specific city and go there in the beginning.

All revenues generated by a theatrical release will help your sales to foreign markets and to ancillary markets such as pay cable, VOD platforms, Netflix, Hulu, etc. It's really worth it if you think you can generate $100,000 to $200,000 in ticket sales, even if you don't make money on the release. I always budget for this potential when putting together my marketing budget. If I end up with a great distribution deal and I don't need it, I can still use it to promote the film or, better yet, start paying back the investors!

When you make a deal with your sales agent, they are usually going to expect money for marketing expenses when they go to AFM, Cannes, etc., so this money could be used for that as well. Money will always be needed for something, so plan ahead as much as you can in the beginning.

When I discussed how to raise money for your film, I mentioned presales. If you've made any presales, especially to foreign markets, leave open the option in your contract for a theatrical release in the US, and allow for your percentage to be raised should the film become a breakout hit. You don't want to be stuck getting only a small amount because you sold it early to secure some funding.

You can work with sites like Tugg and create crowdfunded screenings. It's a novel approach to doing a risk-free theatrical release. The only way the screening will happen is if you sell enough tickets. You don't have to rent the theater; they will do a revenue share with you. If this is successful, especially if you can replicate it in multiple markets, you may get picked up by a distributor and again it can help with you ancillary sales.

Even if you don't get a distribution deal or do any sort of theatrical release, you can still make money off your film. There are literally hundreds of platforms—for example, channels on Roku or Apple TV. (Have you ever scrolled through all of the different options you have besides Netflix?) All of those platforms are looking for content. You're not likely to make much money, but if you can get it there, you can drive people to that platform yourself and increase your revenues. Some of those platforms pay a flat fee, but some will do a revenue share.

You can also upload your film yourself to Vimeo, YouTube, and Amazon Prime. All of these platforms have VOD options. Amazon pays the least, but more people have Amazon Prime and you're more likely to get people to watch it there.

Vimeo has their own on-demand platform. You have to pay to become a pro member, but you can set up your own channel, have trailers and all the other bells and whistles, and keep almost all of the revenues. You can also upload your film to YouTube and do the same or release it for free and use it as a marketing tool for a product. Or, if you have enough subscribers, you can include advertising and generate revenues that way.

You could also do a hybrid release where you open in a few select theaters on the same day your film becomes available on VOD. This is referred to as "day and date," and it is a great way to generate press about your release, get reviews and media buzz, and promote your VOD launch.

In terms of DVD sales and/or digital downloads, Vimeo has a digital download option and an option to market DVDs, as does Amazon. I won't say that DVD is dead, but I think it's on its last few breaths. In my budgets and ROI, I generally don't even include DVD sales in my expected revenues, or if I do, it's very little. It really depends on the film. There are still some diehard DVD owners out there, but they are few and far between.

If you really want to create a DVD or a digital download option, then make sure it has additional features that are enticing. Additional footage/interviews, music/sound track, a director commentary, behind-the-scenes footage—something that the viewer might want to have that isn't included in the original film. You can at least charge a premium for this product. Perhaps a copy of the script or transcripts of complete interviews or a book?

Take some time to check out what other filmmakers are doing. The reality is every day there is something new, cooler, better, and it's almost impossible to be up on everything, especially when it's likely you started your film over a year ago. The industry is changing rapidly and what you planned out when you started may be old-school by the time you're finished.

With as many options as there are to get your film to the audience who wants it, as long as you've made a good film, you're more likely these days to make some money off it. Think globally when thinking about distribution. Is your film something that would be appealing to a foreign market? Not only are all these options available in the US, but most foreign markets also have Netflix, pay cable, or theatrical options. FYI: this is how those big blockbusters really make their money; the US is but one small piece of the profit pie for them. There are revenue-stream possibilities everywhere, so be creative. In the chapter on marketing, I will share other ideas for creating revenues beyond your film itself.

Every step of the way, the process of making a documentary seems to get more difficult. It's true: you've got to have an idea, get access to the people to tell the story, raise the money, film it, edit it, and then distribute it. For those who get it right the first time, this process can take from two to four years, but for most filmmakers, it's more like five to seven years. Be patient and don't give up! You will get there.

CHAPTER 19

Marketing (Traditional, Grassroots, Social)

Regardless of how you distribute your film, you should be ready to market it yourself. The truth is, marketing starts when you begin making the film and often when you begin to seek funding, especially if you're doing a crowdfunding campaign.

Marketing isn't just having a Facebook, Twitter, or Instagram page, although those are important. Marketing happens in multiple spaces: online, on the air (radio and TV), and in print (newspapers, magazines). Marketing happens with strategic partnerships, i.e., groups and organizations you collaborate with to help market your film. Essentially, you want to create an access point to anyone who might be interested in your film. This is why, when creating your business plan, you spent time finding where your audience hangs out. What magazines or newspapers do they read? What is their preferred social media outlet? (There may be multiple, but you should at least have Facebook, Twitter, and Instagram; YouTube and Vimeo channels; and any other social media platforms your audience uses, like chat rooms or Reddit.)

Every successful film has a detailed marketing plan outlining each platform or medium and what will be done in that medium and how much you will allot to spend in that medium. This is as important as the budget for your entire film.

It will be broken down into categories; each category requires a slightly different approach.

Crowdfunding Marketing	
Online:	$
Print:	$
TV/radio:	$
PR firm:	$
Assets:*	$
Festival Marketing Campaign	
Online:	$
Print:	$
TV/radio:	$
PR firm:	$
Assets:	$
Theatrical Marketing	
Online:	$
Print:	$
TV/radio:	$
PR firm:	$
Assets:	$
Digital/VOD Marketing	
Online:	$
Print:	$
TV/radio:	$
PR firm:	$
Assets:	$

*Assets include posters, graphic design, website, trailers, and teasers.

If you're serious about people actually seeing your film and making any of your money back, you need to be serious about marketing and budget accordingly.

Each time you create a plan, you should first ask yourself, What am I selling? What do I want people to do when they see my ad? Donate? Buy a ticket? Click a link? Every piece of marketing you do must have a clear call to action. If you're focusing on a crowdfunding campaign, your goal is to get people to contribute. If your goal is to get them to buy a ticket or click a link to watch the movie, you will need a different kind of ad. I use my Five Ws.

- Who is this ad for?
- What do I want them to do when they see it?
- What format is the ad in (video/meme/poster image)?

The medium it will appear in will determine the next three items.

- When should they see this ad?
- Where is this ad best placed?
- Why am I posting this ad?

Conventional marketing wisdom suggests that a person should see your ad at least three times, which is why it is best to create a campaign that has your ad showing up online, in print, and (if you can afford it) on the radio. FYI: radio advertising is still, by far, one of the most effective ways to reach your audience. You can spend a lot of money and work with local NPR affiliates, or you can even do smaller, local outlets or even podcasts if they reach the people you want. Many smaller stations and podcasts will even invite you on as a guest if you do a campaign with them.

Local newspapers also have an online component. If you choose to do a print ad, be sure to create a campaign that utilizes all the options you can afford: a print ad, an online ad, and (if available) an e-mail blast. Some will do a stand-alone e-mail blast, and some will include you in their weekly newsletter.

Calendar listings are usually free and a great way to help build awareness about your film.

The idea is to get your film in as many places as possible that can directly reach your audience, regardless of whether you're releasing theatrically or doing an online premiere.

If you're releasing in a theater, Fandango offers advertising. You can fill out a request form, and they will need to approve it or check with the theater to see if it lists with Fandango or other online movie-listing sites.

Print advertising is probably the most expensive medium. If you're doing a theatrical release, it's worth it to at least have your film listed in the theater's weekly ad. Los Angeles and other major markets can cost upward of $1,000 to $2,000 for a small ad. If your other campaigns (i.e., social, radio, online) are robust, you may be able to get away with skipping it. Most people don't usually use the newspaper anymore for showtimes. Talk with theaters about what options they can make available to you. They will get a better deal with the newspapers since they have a weekly ad, and often they will have special options available for you to purchase directly from them. Newspapers also have online-only options, which may be a better bet for your budget. Many smaller and local papers will offer you a review if you advertise. They won't tell you this up front, but if you ask them, sometimes they'll offer it. Getting reviews of your film is important. Hopefully, they'll be good ones! It's true a bad review can kill a movie. If this happens, have a legion of friends and family ready to write letters disagreeing with the review.

You may think I'm kidding; however, the reality is, you've got to pull out all the stops when marketing your film. Your friends and family, the crew and cast: have everyone you can ready to promote your film. This is what grassroots marketing is all about. It's probably the least expensive way to market your film, and word of mouth is truly the best marketing tool you have. Enlist as many people as possible to share about your film with their social networks; put up posters in their workplaces or favorite hangouts; blab about the film in chat rooms; be willing to go to events and talk about the film; and visit local universities with postcards at the ready.

This is often referred to as your "street team," and they can be worth their weight in gold. A word about promoting on college campuses: they often have rules about promoting events, so be sure to check with them prior to putting up posters or showing up on campus. If your film is playing close to a university (which, especially if it appeals to that audience, is a great idea), you can pay to hang your posters around campus, and you can connect with professors and possibly speak to their classes. Your job is to promote however you can. It's sort of like running for office: the more babies you kiss and hands you shake, the more people will come to your film. Even after all of your other promotions, an in-person connection makes a huge difference.

Prepare printed materials, postcards, and mini posters, and have everyone you know take them to local coffee shops, hairdressers—wherever they go—and leave them out, on the counter, in the window, on the community boards. To get people to see your film, you want them to see an image of your movie as many times as you can and in as many places as you can. People like to be where the buzz is and if they keep seeing and hearing about your film, they are more likely to show up! This is especially important in the areas where your film is playing. If it's in a theater, I try to open my films in the neighborhoods where there is a big concentration of people likely to want to see my film. Is there a university close by? Or a specialized bookstore, a spiritual center, or someplace else my audience likes to congregate?

Special private screenings or word-of-mouth screenings are especially helpful. Can you screen your film for a group or an organization that will support your film? Showing the film to a hundred or so people who will then go home and share about it, write about it, etc., is the best advertising you can get. You want to get influencers there, people with large lists and a large social media presence, or critics. This is why having a premiere is helpful. It's a great way to promote your film while inviting people who can help spread the word, give them a nice event where they can get some pictures and make themselves look cool in the process. This is where working with your strategic partners can make a difference. If your film is premiering online or on a VOD platform, you can still have a premiere in a theater a week or two beforehand or offer a free screening weekend (or a limited number of days) via the platform to your strategic partners' lists as a way to generate buzz about the film and build your marketing warriors! You can do this via a private Vimeo link if your film is landing on Amazon or Netflix, or if you're doing your own VOD, you can set up a free period directly via Vimeo or YouTube. In addition to giving them access to the film for free, prepare downloads of marketing materials that they can use to promote the film.

This is really important when enlisting others to help market your film. Make it easy for them! Create posts and images they can use and put it on a webpage that they can simply share directly from. The easier you make it to share, the more people will do it.

Social media is a whole beast on its own. The truth is, it's a pay-to-play market. Besides having your crew of social warriors sharing about your film, you're going to need to spend some money for sponsored ads to really make sure you saturate the market for your audience. It takes time to build an engaged social presence. I say *engaged* because it's easy to buy followers or get people to follow you, but it's another thing to keep them paying attention, commenting, sharing, and eventually taking the action (buying a ticket, renting the film) you want them to take.

You will need as many assets as you can create to keep your audience engaged: multiple versions of your trailer, teasers, memes, articles, reviews, events . . . content, content, content. You must promote it daily, multiple times a day. You want to be able to post different content, even if it has the same purpose, on different platforms. You want to utilize all the different features: live video, video, IGTV (Instagram TV), Facebook Premiere, watch parties, etc. All of this can seem overwhelming if you don't plan ahead of time. If you can hire a social media firm, do it.

Build an editorial calendar at least three months prior to your release. Before that, keep your followers in the loop on the progress of your film with production stills, dispatches from the set, film festival appearances, and other milestones. If people are following you while you're still in production, they are interested. Keep them engaged. Once you know the when and how of the release of your film, build a calendar to build excitement! This is also a good time to begin to build your audience. Not only do you want followers on social, but you also really want to try to get them to sign up to your e-mail list. E-mail marketing vacillates between being effective and not effective. I have found that when someone signs up to a list for specific movie, they are truly interested. Don't bombard them with e-mails until a couple of weeks prior to the release. Limit yourself to short update messages once a month until you're ready for your call to action. Do you want them to preorder tickets to the theater? Preorder the film or DVD? Can you give them a special offer for being a part of your list? Having a large e-mail list is appealing to distributors in addition to a large platform. If you can show you've got a following, you're more likely to get a deal.

E-mail is also a great tool to use with your strategic partners. In addition to asking them to share on social media, ask them to share news about your film with their e-mail lists. Having multiple strategic partners can grow your reach from 1,000 to 100,000 pretty quickly. Working with your strategic partners to set up special screening times—or having them agree to sell a certain number of tickets to a specific showtime if you're doing a theatrical—will help you boost your sales without your doing all the work.

Provide everyone who is willing to support your launch with the tools they need: tweets with hashtags and links already created; Facebook posts, again with the correct links, tags, and hashtags; Instagram memes, etc. Make it easy for people to share, and don't be shy! The first days of your launch will be an indicator of how well your marketing is doing. You can always adjust if one aspect isn't delivering. Remember to focus your advertising dollars on the places you know your audience will see your info, and be specific. Especially on social media, the more you can narrow down your demographic for your ads, the better they will perform for you. Set up multiple demographic audiences and watch them over a period of two weeks to see which ad set is working best for you. Try different age ranges and interests. Remember, if you're marketing to a younger audience, it's still relevant to market to their parents.

If you have the budget, hire a PR person and a social media marketing firm. You can usually get a local PR person for a theatrical release for about $5,000 per market or you could spend up to $30,000. Spend what you can—it's worth it. Beyond your advertising and social media, having reviews, articles, and other media hits will help give your film credibility. A social media marketing company will help you create your assets and will help take some of the guesswork out of figuring out what platform to post on, how much, how often, etc. Always check references and look up their previous campaigns. Do they have the ability to grasp who your audience is and how to reach them? Have them write a proposal specific to your film. A reputable company will not ask for thousands of dollars up front.

In addition to social marketing, print, radio, etc., think about other unique ways you can market your film. I've always been impressed with campaigns that think outside the box. *Carrie* created a video that went viral. It looked like a real event, and for a while no one knew it was a promo for the film. Narratives usually win the awards for best marketing campaigns, but that doesn't preclude you from learning from their success. Use your subjects and/or any controversy around your subject. Is your film based on a book? Use the author of the book. By the way, if there isn't already a book about your subject, having one written is not only an additional revenue source, but it's also a marketing tool. (You can literally pull a transcript of your film and add some additional text—voilà, you have a book.) You can either release it a few months before the film to begin to generate buzz about the subject or the day and date.

What other products can you create around your film? Is there a course or additional materials you can create? If your film is educational, don't forget to explore an educational platform. Can your film be shown in schools, universities? This is an entirely different avenue for your film and can become lucrative. Companies like Swank will work with you to license your film in the educational space. Create an educational package that includes instructional materials, talking points, and additional footage or commentary for teachers to use.

If nothing else, can you create your own private screening tour of your film? I have had incredible success booking private screenings via groups and organizations who want to show my films to their members. Many of these groups will pay a flat fee for it or do a revenue share with you. Churches, private companies, and organizations will hold screenings of your film. This is a great place to generate income, especially if you have other products to sell at the event. You're looking to get your film seen and hopefully make your money back.

The trick to marketing is in planning and knowing your audience. Be realistic. Not everyone wants to see your film or be bombarded with ads about it, and you don't want to waste time or money promoting to people who aren't interested. Marketing works best when it's targeted and has a clear call to action. If you know your who, what, when, where, and why, have a clear call to action (buy a ticket, click this link, watch here), and have spent the time to create compelling materials (posters, trailers, teasers, ancillary products, a website), then you should have a successful launch. I say *should,* because ultimately your film will speak for itself. It will either take off or it won't. That's the risk we take when we put ourselves out there. A failure in one platform isn't always the kiss of death for your film. Be ready for round two, three, or even four. If you've done your theatrical release and it didn't work out, that doesn't mean you can't find your audience somewhere else.

Don't get locked into the traditional models. Explore all options!

THE WRAP

SECTION VII

I'M TOLD MY BIRTH WAS FILMED for a documentary on natural childbirth. I can't verify this, and I've never actually seen it. However, the irony that I was literally born into the world of documentary has given me many opportunities to giggle about where my life has led me. Prior to making my first documentary, I spent about fifteen years as a child actress, and when I finally figured out I was a terrible actress, I did what anyone with a love of film would do: I switched to a career behind the camera. Spending most of my childhood on movie sets certainly prepared me for a career in film. I began my career behind the camera on a very low- (and I mean *low*) budget film as a production assistant making about $80 a week and was promoted to production coordinator when I totaled my car with the producer in it. Since I didn't have a car anymore and was still willing to work for $80 a week, they kept me on and gave me a job that didn't require me to drive. To this day, it was probably one of my most favorite experiences working on a film. The film was horrible, but lucky for me, the crew, the producers, and the cast were really there to have fun and make a movie. That feeling is something I've tried to re-create on every project I embark on. Have fun. Filmmaking is hard at every step of the way, and there will be days when you wish you'd become a doctor like your mother wanted you to. I have had entire sets burn down in front of my eyes, actors disappear on a drug binge. I've been asked to leave places and I've had interview subjects storm out of the room. I've lost footage, had footage stolen, and literally been arrested and had my camera confiscated, footage and all. Once, I was working as a production assistant and I had my hands full as I was getting into my car. I put my completed petty cash envelope on the roof, which accounted for about $14,000 worth of expenses, and drove off only to realize this about five hours later. Hmm, now that's a predicament. I flew all the way across the country to film an interview in a remote little town, and at midnight my camera person canceled. I filmed that interview on my phone, and even though it wasn't the best looking footage I had, I got what I needed. After years of mistakes, epic failures, and chaos, I have learned to trust my gut and to remain calm, not panic, to rely on my ability to make things happen and my ability to plan ahead, to think through all the possibilities, and to have a plan for as many of those possibilities that I can come up with. Murphy's Law does sometimes prevail, and shit happens. If you've got a good team and you've planned as best as you can, let go of what you can't control and focus on what you can. You will get to the finish line, it will probably cost more than you thought it would, take longer than you'd hoped, and may not turn out exactly as you planned. Letting go of trying to control every outcome feels counterintuitive. You think you need to be in control of every aspect of your film, but guess what? You can't be and the moment you accept that, the easier it will be when some challenge presents itself.

One of the biggest outcomes you're going to need to let go of is your film's success. Did you win an Academy Award? Did you break box office records? Or did your mom and the rest of your family come to see it and that's about it? Once you have funded it, filmed it, and released it, the rest is up to the audience, and they are an unpredictable bunch. Remember that you're competing in a marketplace where a guy with a dinosaur suit and an iPhone can become an instant success while you spent ten years and all your money on a film that may just flop. That's life in the big city, and it doesn't mean you are a failure. I have had films become a box office success and create an entire industry of self-help, publishing, films, and media platforms, and I have had films so bad, they never saw the light of day. I cherish each one of those experiences. They made me a better person and enriched my life, and I learned a lot about myself and everything I have written in this book. That's my why. I love the experience of making a film; it's my passion and it's fun. Life should be fun. That doesn't mean it will always be easy, yet you should be able to look back on every experience, take the wisdom, find the joy and the gift, and move on to the next.

As I said in the beginning of this book, embarking on this journey of making a documentary (creating any big project, really), is a huge emotional, physical, and financial commitment for yourself, your family, and your team. Be sure to begin with a clear conscience and fully committed to the process, and be ready to fail. There are tons of inspirational stories about people who at first failed and then tried again, only to succeed in a bigger way than they'd even imagined. Your first film might not be "the One." With each film, I've learned something new. And I've literally been doing this since the day I was born.

About the Author

Betsy Chasse is an award-winning filmmaker, bestselling author, changemaker, and mom. Best known as the cowriter, codirector, and producer of the hit film *What the Bleep Do We Know?!*, she also produced the award-winning *Song of the New Earth*, *Pregnant in America*, *Radical Dating* (docuseries), and *The Empty Womb* (short documentary). She has authored multiple books, including *Tipping Sacred Cows* and *What the Bleep Do We Know?!: Discovering the Endless Possibilities to Altering Your Everyday Reality*, in addition to several bestselling compilation books. She is the founder of Rampant Feline Media, a publishing and multimedia company, which supports authors and filmmakers worldwide in bringing their creative visions to life.

Index

Books from Allworth Press

Acting for Film (Second Edition)
by Cathy Haase with foreword by Ian McKellen (6 × 9, 272 pages, paperback, $22.99)

Acting in LA
by Kristina Sexton (5½ × 8¼, 216 pages, paperback, $19.99)

An Actor's Guide: Making It in New York City (Second Edition)
by Glenn Alterman (6 × 9, 344 pages, paperback, $24.95)

An Actor's Guide: Your First Year in Hollywood (Fourth Edition)
by Michael St. Nicholas and Lisa Mulcahy (6 × 9, 316 pages, paperback, $19.99)

The Art of Motion Picture Editing
by Vincent LoBrutto (6 × 9, 280 pages, paperback, $24.95)

The Bare Bones Camera Course for Film and Video (Third Edition)
by Tom Schroeppel (6 × 9, 176 pages, paperback, $14.99)

The Film Appreciation Book
by Jim Piper (6 × 9, 288 pages, paperback, $19.95)

The Filmmaker's Guide to Production Design
by Vincent LoBrutto (6 × 9, 224 pages, paperback, $19.95)

Fund Your Dreams Like a Creative Genius™
by Brainard Carey (6⅛ × 6⅛, 160 pages, paperback, $12.99)

The Health and Safety Guide for Film, TV, and Theater (Second Edition)
by Monona Rossol (6 × 9, 288 pages, paperback, $27.50)

Get the Picture? (Second Edition)
by Jim Piper (6 × 9, 336 pages, paperback, $24.95)

Hollywood Dealmaking (Third Edition)
by Dina Appleton and Daniel Yankelevits (6 × 9, 408 pages, paperback, $24.99)

Independent Film Producing
by Paul Battista (6 × 9, 312 pages, paperback, $24.99)

Leadership in the Performing Arts
by Tobie S. Stein (5½ × 8¼, 252 pages, paperback, $19.99)

A Life in Acting
by Lisa Mulcahy (6 × 9, 192 pages, paperback, $16.95)

Movement for Actors (Second Edition)
Edited by Nicole Potter, Mary Fleischer, and Barbara Adrian (6 × 9, 376 pages, paperback, $22.99)

Starting Your Career as an Actor
by Jason Pugatch (6 × 9, 320 pages, paperback, $19.95)

There's Money Where Your Mouth Is (Fourth Edition)
by Elaine A. Clarke (6 × 9, 360 pages, paperback, $24.99)

VO (Second Edition)
by Harlan Hogan (6 × 9, 256 pages, paperback, $19.95)

To see our complete catalog or to order online, please visit *www.allworth.com*.